The
Art of Shepherding

DAG HEWARD-MILLS

Parchment House

Unless otherwise stated, all Scripture quotations are taken from the King James Version of the Bible.

Excerpts taken from *A Shepherd Looks at Psalm 23*, by W. Phillip Keller. Copyright © 1970, 2007 by W. Phillip Keller. Used by permission of Zondervan. WWW.ZONDERVAN.COM

First published by Lux Verbi.BM (Pty) Ltd. 2010
Published by Parchment House 2011
4th Printing 2014

Find out more about Dag Heward-Mills
Healing Jesus Crusade
Write to: evangelist@daghewardmills.org
Website: www.daghewardmills.org
Facebook: Dag Heward-Mills
Twitter: @EvangelistDag

ISBN: 978-9988-8505-2-4

Dedication
To *Patrick and Joy Bruce*
Thank you for a great work done in northern Ghana.

Contents

Chapter 1

What Makes Sheep
Lie Down

O come, let us worship and bow down: let us kneel before the LORD our maker.

For he is our God; and WE ARE THE PEOPLE OF HIS PASTURE, AND THE SHEEP OF HIS HAND...

Psalm 95:6-7

In the Word of God, His people are called sheep. Jesus described us as "sheep without a shepherd". It is important to understand the life and behaviour of sheep in order to lead them effectively. You must see yourself as a sheep in relation to God and in relation to your pastor. You must also see your church members as sheep in order to understand them better. In the twenty-third Psalm we see how David describes the life of a sheep from his own experience as a shepherd. This vivid description of "sheep life" comes from the mouth of an experienced Israelite shepherd who pictures himself as God's own sheep.

Because the Lord is my Shepherd, I have everything I need!

He lets me rest in the meadow grass and leads me beside the quiet streams. He gives me new strength. He helps me do what honors him the most.

Even when walking through the dark valley of death I will not be afraid, for you are close beside me, guarding, guiding all the way.

You provide delicious food for me in the presence of my enemies. You have welcomed me as your guest; blessings overflow!

Your goodness and unfailing kindness shall be with me all of my life, and afterwards I will live with you forever in your home.

Psalm 23:1-6 (The Living Bible)

1

I was excited to discover many similar parallels in the life of a sheep as revealed by a modern-day shepherd, W. Phillip Keller, who worked for eight years as a sheep owner and sheep rancher in British Columbia. He had the practical experience of shepherding in a modern context and gives amazing confirmation to the revelations of Psalm 23.

The LORD is my shepherd; I shall not want. HE MAKETH ME TO LIE DOWN in green pastures: he leadeth me beside the still waters.

Psalm 23:1-2

Sheep lie down only under certain circumstances. You must be able to make the sheep in your church lie down and stay with you. You must stabilize the frightened sheep and keep people in a family around you. From his experience as a shepherd, Phillip Keller shares a few things that will make the sheep lie down. Each one of the four points below reveals why some people cannot stay in a church. Tension with other members, fear, demonic attacks and lack of good food from the pulpit are all reasons why sheep do not settle down in churches. Phillip Keller says:

1. **Sheep will lie down when they are free from fear:** Owing to their timidity they refuse to lie down unless they are free of all fear. Sheep are so timid and easily panicked that even a stray jackrabbit suddenly bounding from behind a bush can stampede a whole flock. When one startled sheep runs in fright a dozen others will bolt with it in blind fear, not waiting to see what frightened them.

2. **Sheep will lie down when there is no tension with others of their kind:** Because of the social behaviour within a flock, sheep will not lie down unless they are free from friction with others of their kind.

3. **Sheep will lie down when they are not tormented by flies or parasites:** If tormented by flies or parasites sheep will not lie down. Only when free of these pests can they relax.

4. **Sheep will lie down when they are free from hunger:** Sheep will not lie down as long as they feel in need of finding food. They must be free from hunger. To be at rest there must be a definite sense of freedom from fear, tension, aggravations and hunger.[1]

Chapter 2

Why Sheep Need Water

The LORD is my shepherd; I shall not want. He maketh me to lie down in green pastures: HE LEADETH ME BESIDE THE STILL WATERS.

Psalm 23:1-2

Our modern shepherd, Phillip Keller, describes his experiences with sheep and shares how sheep need a lot of water to live normally. He noticed that when the sheep do not get the waters of the Spirit they need, they seek for it in all the wrong places. This teaches us that every shepherd must minister and provide the water of the Holy Spirit for the sheep. Pastors must be spiritual and minister powerfully from the anointing of the Holy Spirit. The lack of anointed ministry from the pulpit is the reason why church members are found seeking solutions from occultic sources and witchcraft power.

Phillip Keller says:

Just as the physical body has a capacity and need for water, so Scripture points out to us clearly that the human soul has a capacity and need for the water of the Spirit of the eternal God. When sheep are thirsty they become restless and set out in search of water. If they are not led to good water *they will often end up drinking from the polluted pot holes* where they pick up internal parasites such as nematodes, liver flukes, and other germs.

They remind me very much of a bunch of sheep I watched one day which were being led down to a magnificent mountain stream. The snow-fed waters were flowing pure and clear and crystal clean between lovely banks of trees. But on the way several stubborn ewes and their lambs stopped, instead, to drink from small, dirty, muddy pools beside the trail. The water was filthy and polluted not only with the churned up mud from the passing sheep but even with the manure and urine of previous flocks that had passed that way. Still these stubborn sheep were quite sure it was the best drink obtainable.

The water itself was filthy and unfit for them. Much more, it was obviously contaminated with nematodes and liver fluke eggs that would eventually riddle them with internal parasites and diseases of destructive impact.

There are three main sources of water for sheep: springs and streams, dew on the grass, and deep wells. The body of an animal such as a sheep is composed of about 70 percent water on an average. Water is used to maintain normal body metabolism; it is a portion of every cell, contributing to its turgidity and normal life functions.

Water therefore determines the vitality, strength and vigour of the sheep.[2]

Chapter 3

What It Means for Sheep to Be Cast Down

Why art thou cast down, O my soul? and why art thou disquieted within me? hope thou in God...

Psalm 42:11

Our modern shepherd also describes his experiences with sheep and shares what it means for a sheep to be cast down. It is interesting to discover how any of the sheep can become helpless and unable to stand on its feet without help. The parallel between real sheep and real people is striking, to say the least.

Phillip Keller shares his experiences as a sheep owner working with real sheep. He says:

Cast or cast down is an old English shepherd's term for a sheep that has turned over on its back and cannot get up again by itself. A cast sheep is a very pathetic sight. Lying on its back, its feet in the air, it flays away frantically struggling to stand up, without success. Sometimes it will bleat a little for help, but generally it lies there lashing about in frightened frustration.

If the owner does not arrive on the scene within a reasonably short time, the sheep will die. This is but another reason why it is so essential for a careful shepherd to look over his flock every day, counting them to see that all are able to be up and on their feet. If one or two are missing, often the first thought to flash into his mind is, *One of my sheep is cast somewhere. I must go in search and set it on its feet again.*

It is not only the shepherd who keeps a sharp eye for cast sheep but also the predators. Buzzards, vultures, dogs, coyotes and cougars all know that a cast sheep is easy prey and death is not far off.

This knowledge that any cast sheep is helpless, close to death and vulnerable to attack makes the whole problem of cast sheep serious for the manager. Nothing seems to so arouse his constant care and diligent attention to the flock as the fact that even the largest, fattest, strongest and sometimes healthiest sheep can become cast and be a casualty. Actually it is often the fat sheep that are the most easily cast.

This is how it happens: A heavy, fat or long-fleeced sheep will lie down comfortably in some little hollow or depression in the ground. It may roll on its side slightly to stretch out or relax. Suddenly the centre of gravity in the body shifts so that it turns on its back far enough that the feet no longer touch the ground. It may feel a sense of panic and start to paw frantically. Frequently this only makes things worse. It rolls over even further. Now it is quite impossible for it to regain its feet.

As it lies there struggling, gases begin to build up in the rumen. As these expand they tend to retard and cut off blood circulation to extremities of the body, especially the legs. If the weather is very hot and sunny, a cast sheep can die in a few hours. If it is cool and cloudy and rainy, it may survive in this position for several days.

A shepherd would spend hours searching for a single sheep that is missing. More often he would see it at a distance, down on its back and lying helpless. He would start to run toward it – hurrying as fast as he can – for every minute is critical. Within the shepherd is a mingled sense of fear and joy: fear that it might be too late; joy that it was found at all.

As soon as the shepherd reaches the cast ewe, his first impulse is to pick it up. Tenderly he would roll the sheep over on its side. This would relieve the pressure of gases in the rumen. If the sheep had been down for long the shepherd would have to lift it onto its feet. Then, straddling the sheep with his legs the shepherd would hold the sheep erect, rubbing its limbs to restore the circulation to its legs. This often took quite a little time. When the sheep started to walk again it often just stumbled, staggered and collapsed in a heap once more.

Little by little the sheep would regain its equilibrium. It would start to walk steadily and surely. By and by it would dash away to rejoin the others, set free from its fears and frustrations, given another chance to live a little longer. Sheep are cast down for different reasons.

1. **The sheep that chose the comfortable, soft, rounded hollows in the ground in which to lie down very often become cast.** In such a situation it is so easy to roll over on their backs.

   In the Christian life there is great danger in always looking for the easy place, the cosy corner, the comfortable position where there is no hardship, no need for endurance, no demand upon self-discipline.

2. **Having too much wool can cause a sheep to be cast down.** Often when the fleece becomes very long and heavily matted with mud, manure, burrs and other debris, it is much easier for a sheep to become cast, literally weighed down with its own wool.

   "Wool" in Scripture depicts the old self-life in the Christian. It is the outward expression of an inner attitude, the assertion of our own desire and hopes and aspirations. It is the area of our lives in which we are continually in contact with the world around us. Here is where we find the clinging accumulation of things, of possessions, of worldly ideas weighing, dragging and holding us down.

   It is significant that no high priest was ever allowed to wear wool when hc entered the Holy of Holies. This spoke of self, pride and personal preference – and God would not tolerate it.

   When a sheep is cast because it has too long and heavy a fleece the shepherd takes swift steps to remedy the situation. He would shear it clean and forestall the danger of having the ewe lose its life. This is not a pleasant process. Sheep do not really enjoy being sheared. It also represents hard work for the shepherd, but it must be done.

3. **Being too fat can cause a sheep to be cast. It is a well-known fact that over-fat sheep are neither the healthiest nor the most productive.** And certainly it is the fattest that most often are cast. Their weight simply makes it that much harder for them to be agile and nimble on their feet. Once a shepherd even suspects that his sheep are becoming cast because they are too fat he takes long-range steps to correct the problem. He puts the ewes on a more rigorous ration: they get less grain and their general condition is watched more closely. The aim of the shepherd is to see that the sheep are strong, sturdy and energetic and not fat, flabby and weak.[3]

Chapter 4

Why Sheep Need Guidance

The LORD is my shepherd; I shall not want. He maketh me to lie down in green pastures: he leadeth me beside the still waters.

He restoreth my soul: HE LEADETH ME in the paths of righteousness for his name's sake.

Psalm 23:1-3

Without guidance our church members would go astray and their lives would be destroyed. Many people have *self-destructive patterns* built into their lives. The modern shepherd reveals how sheep need guidance. He tells us that when sheep are left to themselves they go astray and destroy themselves with negative self-destructive patterns.

He shares:

A commonly held but serious misconception about sheep is that they can just "get along anywhere." The truth is quite the reverse. *No other class of livestock requires more careful handling, more detailed direction than do sheep.* Just as sheep will blindly, habitually and stupidly follow one another along the same little trails until they become ruts that erode into gigantic gullies, so we humans cling to the same habits that we have seen ruin other lives.

All we like sheep have gone astray; we have turned every one to his own way; and the LORD hath laid on him the iniquity of us all.

Isaiah 53:6

Sheep have to be managed and handled with intelligent care. When sheep are left to themselves they go their own way and according to the whims of their own destructive habits.

1. **Without guidance sheep would follow the same trails until they became ruts.** The sheep would gnaw the grass to the very ground until even the roots are damaged. In such places, the grass roots are pawed out of the soil, leaving utter barrenness behind. Such abuse means loss of fertility and the exposure of the land to all ravages of erosion.

2. **Without guidance sheep would graze the same hills until they turned into desert wastes.** Both land and owner are ruined while the sheep become thin, wasted and sickly. The greatest single safeguard which a shepherd has in handling his flock is to keep them on the move. They must be shifted from pasture to pasture periodically.

3. **Without guidance sheep would pollute their own ground until it was corrupt with disease and parasites.** Because of the behaviour of sheep and their preference for certain favoured spots, these well-worn areas become quickly invested with parasites of all kinds. In a short time a whole flock can thus become infested with worms, nematodes and scab.[4]

Seven Signs That You Are Following a Shepherd

1. Prosperity. The first sign that you are being led by a shepherd is prosperity. Prosperity always comes to someone who obeys the voice of the Lord.

   The LORD is my shepherd; I SHALL NOT WANT.

   Psalms 23:1

2. Calmness. The second sign that you are being led by a shepherd is calmness, restfulness and assurance.

   ...he leadeth me beside the STILL WATERS.

   Psalms 23:2

3. Spiritual food. Someone who is under the care of a shepherd is filled with the Word of God.

He maketh me to lie down in GREEN PASTURES...

Psalms 23:2

4. Comfort. Receiving comfort is another blessing of being close to your shepherd.

Yea, though I walk through the valley of the shadow of death, I will fear no evil: for thou art with me; THY ROD AND THY STAFF THEY COMFORT ME.

Psalms 23:4

5. Anointing. People who follow the shepherd become anointed. The anointing is a sign that you are truly following the Lord.

...thou ANOINTEST MY HEAD with oil; my cup runneth over.

Psalms 23:5

6. Goodness and mercy. If you are following the shepherd you must expect good things and merciful things to abound in your life. Goodness and mercy in your life is a sign that you are following the shepherd.

Surely goodness and mercy shall follow me all the days of my life...

Psalms 23:6

7. Eternal joy. Eternal joy is the portion of those who follow the shepherd.

.... I will dwell in the house of the LORD for ever.

Psalms 23:6

Chapter 5

Why Sheep Need
Green Pastures

The LORD is my shepherd; I shall not want. He maketh me to lie down in green pastures: he leadeth me beside the still waters.

Psalm 23:1-2

Once again, our modern shepherd describes how sheep need fresh pastures to graze on. He describes how the reputation of the shepherd is determined by how he is able to arrange different feeding pastures for the sheep. He says and I quote:

There must be a predetermined plan of action; a deliberate planned rotation from one grazing ground to another in line with right and proper principles of sound management. The owner's name and reputation depends on how effectively and efficiently he keeps his charges moving onto wholesome, new and fresh forage. That is what David had in mind when he spoke of being led in paths of righteousness.

A shepherd must have an intimate knowledge of his pastures. He must be all over the grounds again and again. He must know every advantage and every drawback. He must know where his flock will thrive and be aware of where the feed is poor so he knows where to guide the sheep to. Whenever a shepherd opens a gate into a fresh pasture the sheep are filled with excitement. As they go through the gate even the staid old ewes will often kick up their heels and leap with delight at the prospect of finding fresh feed. How they enjoy being led onto new ground!

In my mind's eye I can see my flock again. The gentleness, stillness and the softness of early morning always found my sheep knee-deep in dew-drenched grass. There they fed heavily and contentedly. As the sun rose and its heat burned the dewdrops from the leaves, the flock would retire to find shade. There, fully satisfied and happily refreshed, they would lie down to rest and ruminate through the day. Nothing pleased me more.[5]

Chapter 6

Why Sheep Need to Go
through Valleys

Yea, THOUGH I WALK THROUGH THE VALLEY
of the shadow of death, I will fear no evil: for thou art
with me; thy rod and thy staff they comfort me.

Psalm 23:4

Our modern shepherd also describes his experiences with sheep and shares how sheep need to be taken through valleys. It is interesting to note that shepherds do not only lead their sheep through the high ground but also take them through valleys. Many of us think that if God is with us He will lead us only on the high ground. But a valley speaks of the low times and low seasons of our lives.

We learn how the shepherd does not leave the sheep in valleys but leads them through the dark and frightening valleys and back to the high ground. Is this not a description of our very own lives? How many times have we been through dark and lonely valleys when it was only the voice of the shepherd that sustained us? How many times have church members depended on the reassurance and strength of their pastor?

Once again, I quote from the experiences of a real hands-on shepherd who had the experience of practising real shepherding techniques.

He says:

1. **Most of the efficient shepherds endeavour to take their flocks onto distant ranges during summer.** This often entails long "drives". The sheep move along slowly, feeding as they go, gradually working their way up the mountains behind the receding snow. By late summer they are well up on the remote alpine meadows above the timberline.

With the approach of autumn, early snow settles on the highest ridges, relentlessly forcing the flock to withdraw down to lower elevations. Finally, toward the end of the year as fall passes, the sheep are driven home to the ranch headquarters where they will spend the winter.

During this time, the flock is entirely alone with the shepherd. They are in intimate contact with him and under his most personal attention day and night.

Every mountain has valleys. Its sides are scarred by deep ravines and gulches and draws. And the best route to the top is always along these valleys. Any shepherd familiar with the high country knows this. He leads his flock gently, but persistently, up the paths that wind through the dark valleys. It should be noticed that the verse states, "Even though I *walk through* the valley of the shadow of death." It does not say I die there, or stop there- but rather "I walk through."

2. **It is in the valleys of our lives that we find refreshment from God Himself.** It is not until we have walked with Him through some very deep troubles that we discover He can lead us to find our refreshment in Him right there in the midst of our difficulty. Unless one has actually gone through such an experience it may seem difficult to believe.

3. **Only those who have been through such dark valleys can console, comfort and encourage others in similar situations.** Most of us do not want valleys in our lives. We shrink from them with a sense of fear and foreboding. Yet in spite of our worst misgivings God can bring great benefit and lasting benediction to others through those valleys.

4. **A shepherd chooses to take his flock through the valleys because generally the richest feed and best forage are found along the route.** The flock is moved along gently – they are not hurried. The lambs have never been this way before. The shepherd wants to be sure there will not only be water but also the best grazing available for the ewes

and their lambs. Generally the choicest meadows are in
these valleys along the stream banks. Here the sheep can
feed as they move toward the high country.[6]

Chapter 7

What It Means for Sheep
to Be Discontented

The modern shepherd describes how real sheep can be discontented and cause trouble for the rest of the flock. The description of real sheep causing division, discontentment and confusion teaches every shepherd not to be surprised by similar manifestations in "human sheep". Indeed, the way a real shepherd deals with confusion-causing sheep is a revelation for all pastors – execute the disloyal sheep and eat them for supper!

Let's learn from a modern shepherd. Here is another excerpt from the book, *A Shepherd Looks at Psalm 23:*

"Behold, he that keepeth Israel shall neither slumber nor sleep" (Psalm 121:4).

In spite of having such a master and owner, the fact remains that some Christians are still not content with His control. They are somewhat dissatisfied, always feeling that somehow the grass beyond the fence must be a little greener. These are carnal Christians – one might almost call them "fence crawlers" or "half-Christians" who want the best of both worlds.

I once owned an ewe whose conduct exactly typified this sort of person. She was one of the most attractive sheep that ever belonged to me. Her body was beautifully proportioned. She had a strong constitution and an excellent coat of wool. Her head was clean, alert, well-set with bright eyes. She bore sturdy lambs that matured rapidly. But in spite of all these attractive attributes she had one pronounced fault. She was restless – discontent – a fence crawler.

This one ewe produced more problems for me than almost all the rest of the flock combined. No matter what field or pasture the sheep were in, she would search all along the fences or

18

shoreline (we lived by the sea) looking for a loophole she could crawl through and start to feed on the other side. It was not that she lacked pasturage. My fields were my joy and delight. No sheep in the district had better grazing.

With this sheep it was an ingrained habit. She was simply never contented with things as they were. Often when she had forced her way through some such spot in a fence or found a way around the end of the wire at low tide on the beaches, she would end up feeding on bare, brown, burned-up pasturage of a most inferior sort. But she never learned her lesson and continued to fence crawl time after time.

Now it would have been bad enough if she was the only one who did this. It was a sufficient problem to find her and bring her back. But the further point was that she taught her lambs the same tricks. They simply followed her example and soon were as skilled at escaping as their mother.

Even worse, however, was the example she set for the other sheep. In short time she began to lead others through the same holes and over the same dangerous paths down by the sea.

After putting up with her perverseness for a summer, I finally came to the conclusion that to save the rest of the flock from becoming unsettled, she would have to go. I could not allow one obstinate, discontented ewe to ruin the whole ranch operation.

It was a difficult decision to make, for I loved her in the same way I loved the rest. Her strength and beauty and alertness were a delight to the eye.

But one morning I took the killing knife in hand and butchered her. Her career of fence crawling was cut short. It was the only solution to the dilemma. She was a sheep, who, in spite of all that I had done to give her the very best care, still wanted something else.[7]

Chapter 8

Why the Sheep
Need a Rod

Yea, though I walk through the valley of the shadow of death, I will fear no evil: for thou art with me; THY ROD and thy staff they COMFORT ME.

Psalm 23:4

Phillip Keller, a modern shepherd describes how the rod is the main equipment of the shepherd. The rod therefore speaks of the Word of God which is used to deal with men. It is the only basis of power and authority of the shepherd. A pastor must treasure the Word of God and see it as his greatest tool in the ministry. The Word of God does for the pastor what the rod does for the shepherd:

1. The rod is what the shepherd relies on to safeguard both himself and his flock in danger.

2. The rod is the instrument the shepherd uses to discipline and correct any wayward sheep that insists on wandering away.

3. The shepherd's rod is his weapon of power and authority.

4. There is comfort and consolation in seeing the rod in the shepherd's skilful hands. The sheep asserts that the shepherd's rod is a continuous comfort to him.

5. The rod is used by the shepherd for the welfare of his sheep – to discipline the sheep.

6. The shepherd uses the rod to examine and count the sheep. "And I will cause you to pass under the rod, and I will bring you into the bond of the covenant" (Ezekiel 20:37). To come "under the rod" means to come under the shepherd's control and authority; to be subject to the shepherd's most

careful, intimate and first-hand examination. When a sheep passed "under the rod" it meant it had been counted and looked over with great care to make sure that all was well with it.

7. The shepherd's rod is an instrument of protection for both himself and his sheep when they are in danger. It is used both as a defence and a deterrent against anything that would attack.[8]

Chapter 9

Why the Sheep
Need a Staff

**Yea, though I walk through the valley of the shadow
of death, I will fear no evil: for thou art with me; THY
ROD and thy staff they COMFORT ME.**

Psalm 23:4

Our modern shepherd describes the difference between the
staff and the rod. He tells us that whereas the rod conveys
the concept of authority, power and discipline and defence
against danger, the staff speaks of all that is longsuffering and
kind. The shepherd's staff is a long, slender stick, often with a
crook or hook on one end. It is selected with care by the owner.
It is shaped, smoothed and cut to best suit the shepherd's own
personal use. The staff is a symbol of comfort and concern. It
demonstrates the compassion the shepherd has for his sheep.

Philip Keller says:

Being stubborn creatures, sheep often get into the most
ridiculous and preposterous dilemmas. I have seen my own
sheep, greedy for one more mouthful of green grass, climb
down steep cliffs where they slipped and fell into the sea.
Only my long shepherd's staff could lift them out of the
water back unto solid ground again. One winter day I spent
several hours rescuing an ewe that had done this very thing
several times before. Her stubbornness was her undoing.

Another common occurrence was to find sheep stuck fast in
labyrinths of wild roses or brambles where they had pushed
in to find a few stray mouthfuls of green grass. Soon the
thorns were so hooked in their wool they could not possibly
pull free, tug as they might. Only the use of a staff could free
them from their entanglement.

Likewise with us. Many of our jams and impasses are of our own making. In stubborn, self-willed self-assertion we keep pushing ourselves into a situation where we cannot extricate ourselves. Then in tenderness, compassion, and care our Shepherd comes to us. He draws near and in tenderness lifts us by His Spirit out of the difficulty and dilemma. What patience God has with us! What longsuffering and compassion! What forgiveness!

Your staff comforts me! Your Spirit, O Christ is my consolation!

1. **The shepherd uses the staff to draw the sheep together into an intimate relationship.** The shepherd will use his staff to gently lift a newborn lamb and bring it to its mother if they become separated. He does this because he does not wish to have the ewe reject her offspring if it bears the odour of his hands upon it.

2. **The staff is used by the shepherd to reach out and catch individual sheep, young or old and draw them close to himself for intimate examination.** The staff is very useful this way for the shy and timid sheep that normally tend to keep at a distance from the shepherd.

3. **A shepherd often uses his staff to guide his sheep gently into a new path, through some gate or along dangerous, difficult routes.** He does not use it to beat the sheep. Rather the tip of the staff is laid gently against the sheep's side and the pressure applied guides the sheep in the way the owner wants it to go. This reassures the sheep of its proper path.[9]

Chapter 10

What It Means for Sheep to Have a Table in the Presence of Enemies

It is a reality that our lives are being lived out in the presence of the enemy. Satan is our enemy and he is looking for a foothold, an opportunity to strike at us. It is uncanny to think that your every move is being watched. At home, in the privacy of your room, when you are watching television, those evil eyes are trained on you. This is the portion of everyone who lives on this earth. Your enemy can see you but you cannot see him! It is the duty of the shepherd to watch out for the very lives of the sheep. It is only a good shepherd whose vigilance will save the lives of the sheep.

Philip Keller, a man who learnt the art of shepherding first-hand has this to say:

Another task the attentive shepherd takes on in the summer is to keep an eye out for predators. He will look for signs and spoor of wolves, coyotes, cougars, and bears. If these raid or molest the sheep, he will have to hunt them down or go to great pains to trap them so that his flock can rest in peace.

Often what actually happens is that these crafty ones are up on the rimrock watching every movement the sheep make, hoping for a chance to make a swift, sneaking attack that will stampede the sheep. Then one of the flock is bound to fall easy prey to the attacker's fierce teeth and claws.

The picture here is full of drama, action, suspense - and possible death. Only the alertness of the sheepman who tends his flock on the tableland in full view of possible enemies can prevent them from falling prey to attack. It is only his preparation for such an eventuality that can possibly save the sheep from being slaughtered and panicked by their predators.

And again we are given a sublime picture of our Saviour who knows every wile, every treachery of our enemy Satan and his companions. Always we are in danger of attack. Scripture sometimes refers to him as "a roaring lion" who goes about seeking whom he may devour.

It is rather fashionable in some contemporary Christian circles to discredit Satan. There is a tendency to try and write him off or laugh him off as though he were just a joke. Some deny that such a being as Satan even exists. Yet we see evidence of his merciless attacks and carnage in society where men and women fall prey to his cunning tactics every day. We see lives torn and marred and seared by his assaults though we may never see him personally.

It reminds me of my encounters with cougars. On several occasions these cunning creatures came in among my sheep at night working terrible havoc in the flock. Some ewes were killed outright, their blood drained and livers eaten. Others were torn open and badly clawed. In these cases the great cats seemed to chase and play with them in their panic like a housecat would chase a mouse. Some had huge patches of wool torn from their fleeces. In their frightened stampede some had stumbled and broken bones or rushed over rough ground injuring legs and bodies.

Yet despite the damage, despite the dead sheep, despite the injuries and fear instilled in the flock, I never once actually saw a cougar on my range. So cunning and so skilful were their raids that they defy description.

At all times we would be wise to walk a little closer to Christ. This is one sure place of safety. It was always the distant sheep, the roamers, the wanderers that were picked off by the predators in an unsuspecting moment. Generally the attackers are gone before the shepherd is alerted by their cry for help. Some sheep, of course, are utterly dumb with fear under attack; they will not even give a plaintive bleat before their blood is spilled.

The same is true of Christians. Many of us get into deep difficulty beyond ourselves; we are stricken dumb with apprehension, unable even to call or cry out for help; we just crumple under our adversary's attack.[10]

Chapter 11

Why Sheep Need to Be
Anointed with Oil

**...THOU ANOINTEST MY HEAD WITH OIL; my
cup runneth over.**

Psalm 23:5

Modern shepherding techniques also demonstrate the
importance of being anointed. The anointing oil of the
shepherd is used to rub the sheep. The anointing oil wards off
flies and heals wounds. The flies speak of evil spirits that afflict
our church members. The wounds come from the experiences
that people have in this life.

The people desperately need to be free from the demons that
afflict, accuse and tempt them continually. The people need to be
healed of the bitter experiences of this life.

Only the anointing of the Holy Spirit can do this work in our
hearts. Amazingly, our modern shepherd once again reveals how
the anointing is put to work practically to fight flies and to heal
the wounds of sheep.

1. How the Anointing Oil Fights Flies and
Other Insects

In the terminology of the shepherd "summertime is fly time."
By this, reference is made to the hordes of insects that emerge
with the advent of warm weather. Only those people who
have kept livestock or studied wildlife habits are aware of
the serious problems for animals presented by insects in the
summer.

To name just a few parasites that trouble stock and make their
lives a misery: there are warble flies, bot flies, heel flies,

(nose) nasal flies, deer flies, black flies, mosquitoes, gnats and other minute winged parasites that proliferate at this time of year. Their attacks on animals can readily turn the golden summer months into a time of torture for sheep and drive them almost to distraction.

Sheep are especially troubled by the nose fly, or nasal fly, as it is sometimes called. These little flies buzz about the sheep's head, attempting to deposit their eggs on the damp mucous membranes of the sheep's nose. If they are successful, the eggs will hatch in a few days to form small, slender, worm-like larvae. They work their way up the nasal passages into the sheep's head; they burrow into the flesh and there set up an intense irritation accompanied by severe inflammation.

For relief from this agonizing annoyance sheep will deliberately beat their heads against trees, rocks, posts or brush. They will rub them in the soil and thrash around against woody growth. In extreme cases of intense infestation a sheep may even kill itself in a frenzied endeavour to gain respite from the aggravation. Often advanced stages of infection from these flies will lead to blindness.

Because of all this when the nose flies hover around the flock some of the sheep become frantic with fear and panic in their attempt to escape their tormentors. They will stamp their feet erratically and race from place to place in the pasture trying desperately to elude the flies. They will hide in any bush or woodland that offers shelter. On some occasions they may refuse to graze in the open at all.

Only the strictest attention to the behaviour of the sheep by the shepherd can forestall the difficulties of "fly time." *At the very first sign of flies among the flock he will apply an antidote to their heads. A remedy composed of linseed oil, sulphur and tar was smeared over the sheep's nose and head as a protection against nose flies.*

What an incredible transformation this would make among the sheep. Once the oil had been applied to the sheep's head there was an immediate change in behaviour. Gone was the aggravation, gone the frenzy, gone the irritability and the restlessness. Instead, the sheep would feed quietly again, then soon lie down in peaceful contentment.

Just as with the sheep, there must be a continuous and renewed application of oil to forestall the "flies" in my life; there must be a continuous anointing of God's gracious Spirit to counteract the ever-present aggravations of personality conflicts.

Only one application of oil, sulphur and tar was not enough for the entire summer. It was a process that had to be repeated. The fresh application was the effective antidote.

It is the daily anointing of God's gracious Spirit upon my mind which produces in my life such personality traits as joy, contentment, love, patience, gentleness and peace. What a contrast this is to the tempers, frustration and irritableness which mar the daily conduct of so many of God's children.

2. How the Anointing Oil Heals Wounds

Summertime for the sheep is more than just fly time. It is also "scab time." Scab is an irritating and highly contagious disease common among sheep the world over. Caused by a minute microscopic parasite that proliferates in warm weather, "scab" spreads throughout a flock by direct contact between infected and non-infected animals. Scab is most commonly found around the head. Sheep love to rub heads in an affectionate and friendly manner. When two sheep rub together, the infection spreads readily from one to the other.

In the Old Testament when it was declared that the sacrificial lambs should be without blemish, the thought uppermost in the writer's mind was that the animal should be free of scab. In a very real and direct sense scab is significant of contamination of sin and of evil.

As with flies, the only effective antidote is to apply linseed oil, sulphur and other chemicals that control this disease. In

Palestine the old remedy for this disease was olive oil mixed with sulphur and spices.

In many sheep-rearing countries dips are built and the entire flock is put through the dip. Each animal is completely submerged in the solution until its entire body is soaked. The most difficult part to do is the head. The head has to be plunged under repeatedly to insure that scab there will be controlled. Some shepherds take great care to treat the head by hand."

Chapter 12

Why Sheep Need
the Shepherd's Cup to Overflow

**... thou anointest my head with oil; MY CUP
RUNNETH OVER.**

Psalm 23:5

I did not know that a shepherd has a literal cup until I learnt it
from a real shepherd who carried a bottle containing a mixture
of brandy and water. This shepherd's mixture of brandy and water
overflowed into a blessing of healing and restoration for freezing
sheep that were distressed by extreme weather. The overflowing
cup of the shepherd was a life-giving cup to the sheep.

Indeed, our Lord Jesus' blood overflowed to bring salvation
and healing to the whole world. The cup of every pastor must
overflow to bring life and healing to needy sheep. Phillip Keller,
an experienced shepherd, tells us how he practically ministered
to sheep from his "overflowing cup".

He says:

Blizzards can blow up or sleet storms suddenly shroud the
hills. The flock and their owner can pass through appalling
suffering together.

It is here that I grasp another aspect altogether of the meaning
of a cup that overflows. There is in every life a cup of
suffering. Jesus Christ referred to His agony in the garden
of Gethsemane and at Calvary as His cup. And had it not
overflowed with His life poured out for men, we would have
perished.

In tending my sheep I carried a bottle in my pocket containing
a mixture of brandy and water. Whenever a ewe or lamb was
chilled from undue exposure to wet, cold weather I would
pour a few spoonfuls down his throat. In a matter of minutes

the chilled creature would be on its feet and full of renewed energy. It was especially cute the way the lambs would wiggle their tails with joyous excitement as the warmth from the brandy spread through their bodies.

The important thing was for me to be there on time, to find the frozen, chilled sheep before it was too late. I had to be in the storm with them, alert to every one that was in distress. Some of the most vivid memories of my sheep ranching days are wrapped around the awful storms my flock and I went through together.

I can see again the gray-black banks of storm clouds sweeping in off the sea; I can see the sleet and hail and snow sweeping across the hills; I can see the sheep racing for shelter in the tall timber; I can see them standing there soaked, chilled, and dejected. Especially the young lambs went through appalling misery without the benefit of a full, heavy fleece to protect them. Some would succumb and lie down in distress only to become more cramped and chilled. Then it was that my mixture of brandy and water came to their rescue. I'm sure the Palestine shepherds must have likewise shared their wine with their chilled and frozen sheep.

What a picture of my Master, sharing the wine, the very life blood of His own suffering from His overflowing cup, poured out at Calvary for me. He is there with me in every storm. My Shepherd is alert to every approaching disaster that threatens His people. He has been through the storms of suffering before. He bore our sorrows and was acquainted with our grief.[12]

Chapter 13

Why Sheep Need to Dwell in the House of the Shepherd

... and I WILL DWELL IN THE HOUSE OF THE LORD for ever.

Psalm 23:6

D welling in the house of the Lord speaks of living under the care of the Lord wherever it may be. Whether in the mountains or the valleys, once we are under the keeper's protection we are in the house of the Lord. There is a difference between sheep who are cared for by a good shepherd and those who are under the care of a wicked and uncaring shepherd. Philip Keller gives a vivid illustration of this reality from his own experiences as a shepherd:

> I can never meditate on this last phrase in the Psalm without there welling up in my memory vivid scenes from some of the early days on my first sheep ranch.
>
> As winter, with its cold rains and chilling winds came on, my neighbour's sickly sheep would stand huddled at the fence, their tails to the storm, facing the rich fields in which my flock flourished. *Those poor, abused, neglected creatures under the ownership of a heartless rancher had known nothing but suffering most of the year. With them there had been gnawing hunger all summer. They were thin and sickly with disease and scab and parasites. Tormented by flies and attacked by predators, some were so weak and thin and wretched that their thin legs could scarcely bear their scanty frames.*
>
> Always there seemed to lurk in their eyes the slender, faint hope that perhaps with a bit of luck they could break through the fence or crawl through some hole to free themselves. Occasionally this used to happen, especially around Christmas. This was the time of extreme tides when the sea retreated far out beyond the end of the fence lines which ran

down to it. The neighbour's emaciated, dissatisfied, hungry sheep would wait for this to happen. Then at the first chance they would go down on the tidal flats, slip around the end of the fence and come sneaking in to gorge themselves on our rich green grass.

So pitiful and pathetic was their condition that their the sudden feast of lush feed, to which they were unaccustomed often proved disastrous. Their digestive systems would begin to scout, and sometimes this led to death. I clearly recall coming across three of my neighbour's ewes lying helpless under a fir tree near the fence one drizzly day. They were like three old, limp, gray, sodden sacks collapsed in a heap. Even their bony legs would no longer support them.

I loaded them into a wheelbarrow and wheeled them back to their heartless owner. He simply pulled out a sharp killing knife and slit all three of their throats. He couldn't care less. What a picture of Satan who holds ownership over so many.

Right there the graphic account Jesus portrayed of Himself as being the door and entrance by which sheep were to enter His fold flashed across my mind. Those poor sheep had not come into my ranch through the proper gate. I had never let them in. They had never really become mine. They had not come under my ownership or control. If they had, they would not have suffered so.

Likewise with those apart from Christ. The old world is a pretty wretched ranch and Satan is a heartless owner. He cares not a whit for men's souls or welfare. Under his tyranny there are hundreds of hungry, discontented hearts who long to enter into the household of God – who ache for His care and concern.[13]

Chapter 14

What It Means for the Sheep to Have No Shepherd

1. **AIMLESSNESS:** People are aimless and without direction when there is no shepherd to lead them out and bring them in.

And Moses spake unto the LORD, saying, Let the LORD, the God of the spirits of all flesh, set a man over the congregation, Which may go out before them, and which may go in before them, and WHICH MAY LEAD THEM OUT, AND WHICH MAY BRING THEM IN; THAT THE CONGREGATION OF THE LORD BE NOT AS SHEEP WHICH HAVE NO SHEPHERD.

Numbers 27:15-17

2. **DIVISION:** People are divided and without a family when there is no shepherd.

And he said, I SAW ALL ISRAEL SCATTERED UPON THE HILLS, AS SHEEP THAT HAVE NOT A SHEPHERD: and the LORD said, These have no master: let them return every man to his house in peace.

1 Kings 22:17

3. **WEAKNESS AND DISEASE:** People are diseased and weakened without a shepherd.

THE DISEASED HAVE YE NOT STRENGTHENED, NEITHER HAVE YE HEALED THAT WHICH WAS SICK, neither have ye bound up that which was broken, neither have ye brought again that which was driven away, neither have ye sought that which was lost; but with force and with cruelty have ye ruled them. And they were scattered, because there is no shepherd: and they became meat to all the beasts of the field, when they were scattered. My sheep wandered through all the mountains, and upon every high hill: yea, my flock was scattered upon all the face of the earth, and none did search or seek after them.

Ezekiel 34:4-6

4. **UNSOLVED TROUBLES: People have a lot of unsolved troubles when there is no shepherd.**

For the idols have spoken vanity, and the diviners have seen a lie, and have told false dreams; they comfort in vain: therefore they went their way as a flock, THEY WERE TROUBLED, BECAUSE THERE WAS NO SHEPHERD.

Zechariah 10:2

5. **DESTRUCTION OF YOUNG PEOPLE: The little ones and the young ones are most affected by the absence of the shepherd.**

Awake, O sword, against my shepherd, and against the man that is my fellow, saith the LORD of hosts: smite the shepherd, and the sheep shall be scattered: and I WILL TURN MINE HAND UPON THE LITTLE ONES.

Zechariah 13:7

6. **LACK AND SHORTAGE: People's needs are not met when there is no shepherd.**

The Lord is my shepherd; I SHALL NOT WANT.

Psalm 23:1

7. **GOING OFF COURSE: Sheep need direction to stay on the course of prosperity and blessing for their lives. Sheep receive much direction for their lives through shepherds.**

Thou leddest thy people like a flock by the hand of Moses and Aaron.

Psalm 77:20

Give ear, O Shepherd of Israel, thou that leadest Joseph like a flock; thou that dwellest between the cherubims, shine forth.

Psalm 80:1

Chapter 15

Diseases of Shepherds
Which Are Diseases of Sheep

There are occupational hazards in every field of endeavour. In hospitals, doctors often acquire the diseases of their patients. Sometimes the doctor even dies from the patients' diseases. Likewise, many shepherds acquire the diseases of sheep. Sometimes, the shepherds suffer from more severe variants of illnesses of the sheep.

This is because "shepherds" are also "sheep". All "shepherd" pastors are under the lordship and leadership of the chief shepherd Jesus Christ. This is what makes shepherds also sheep.

Most shepherds and pastors are usually submitted to the leadership of other ministers. Because they must submit and follow, shepherds suffer from the same problems that sheep do. As I have said already, some shepherds even have more serious "sheep diseases" than the sheep themselves.

Seven Diseases of Shepherds
Which Are Diseases of Sheep

1. Weariness

But when He saw the multitudes, He was moved with compassion for them, because they were WEARY and scattered, like sheep having no shepherd.
Matthew 9:36 (NKJV)

Weariness is one of the diseases of sheep. Weariness is equally a disease of shepherds. One of the strategies of the devil is to wear out the saints and make them tired. "And he shall speak great words against the most High, AND SHALL WEAR OUT THE SAINTS of the most High, and think to change times and laws: and they shall be given into his hand until a time and times and the dividing of time" (Daniel 7:25).

2. Aimlessness

Aimlessness is a disease of sheep without their shepherd. Shepherds can likewise become aimless because they no longer follow the guidance of the chief shepherd. Many pastors take their eyes off the great shepherd and begin to follow ideas of men. This is why you find pastors in politics, business, social work and other man-pleasing ventures. It is important for both shepherds and sheep to follow the voice of the Lord. May you be delivered from aimlessness.

When He looked out over the crowds, his heart broke. So confused and AIMLESS they were, like sheep with no shepherd.

Matthew 9:36 (Message Bible)

Where there is no vision, the people perish: but he that keepeth the law, happy is he.

Proverbs 29:18

3. Fainting

But when he saw the multitudes, he was moved with compassion on them, because they FAINTED, and were scattered abroad, as sheep having no shepherd.

Matthew 9:36

Many sheep faint and are no longer able to walk on. Sometimes they have to be carried and sometimes they have to be slaughtered. In our context, fainting happens when the shepherd leaves the ministry: he has fainted or he has stopped the work of ministry.

The Scripture makes it clear that sheep faint because they do not have a shepherd. Seeking the face of the Lord will strengthen you so that you do not have to faint. The presence and influence of a shepherd in your life is the one thing that can keep you from fainting.

4. Scattering

But when he saw the multitudes, he was moved with compassion on them, because they fainted, and were SCATTERED abroad, as sheep having no shepherd.
Matthew 9:36

Many sheep are scattered because they have no shepherd. Shepherds equally become dispersed and do not belong to any family or grouping. If you are led by the Holy Spirit you will definitely hear God telling you to be part of some larger body. Even if you are an independent minister, you will benefit immensely by belonging to other groups and fellowships. I enjoy some of the greatest blessings of my ministry because I am deeply connected to other spiritual groups.

5. Distress

Seeing the people, He felt compassion for them, because they were DISTRESSED and dispirited like sheep without a shepherd.
Matthew 9:36 (NASB)

All kinds of distressing situations come to the lives of God's servants. Being a pastor does not insulate you from these realities. However, having a shepherd in your life will definitely help you through the distressing times of ministry. David was distressed on many occasions. There were times he was surrounded by his enemies. On many occasions, he was in critical danger.

He cried:

They surrounded me, yes, they surrounded me; in the name of the LORD I will surely cut them off. THEY SURROUNDED ME LIKE BEES; they were extinguished as a fire of thorns; in the name of the LORD I will surely cut them off.
Psalm 118:11-12 (NASB)

But in his distress he called on his shepherd. The Lord was his shepherd and the Lord helped him.

FROM MY DISTRESS I CALLED UPON THE LORD; The LORD answered me and set me in a large place. The LORD is for me; I will not fear;

Psalm 118:5-6 (NASB)

6. Confusion

As you go higher in the ministry, confusion will become one of your dreaded enemies. During times of confusion, you will ask the question, "Is this right or is this wrong?" When you are affected by the spirit of confusion, you will grapple with what I call "grey areas". You will wrestle with issues which are not clearly spelt out in the Bible. You will be uncertain of yourself and need great faith to proceed. You will become like the patriarchs of old who had no Bibles guiding them but had to walk by the faith of what they believed God had told them.

Indeed, at such times of confusion, a shepherd's direction would be the most calming and reassuring thing you could have. You will only understand what I am talking about when you get to that stage.

When He looked out over the crowds, his heart broke. So CONFUSED and aimless they were, like sheep with no shepherd.

Matthew 9:36 (Message Bible)

Your confusion is perpetuated by your separation from your shepherd. Because Israel had sinned, they were perpetually separated from the Lord and this created even more confusion for them. Daniel said, "...to us belong confusion of faces because we have sinned."

O Lord, righteousness belongeth unto thee, but UNTO US CONFUSION OF FACES, as at this day; to the men of Judah, and to the inhabitants of Jerusalem, and unto all Israel, that are near, and that are far off, through all the countries whither thou hast driven them, because of their trespass that they have trespassed against thee. O Lord, to us belongeth confusion of face, to our kings,

**to our princes, and to our fathers, because we have
sinned against thee.**

Daniel 9:7-8

Draw close to the Lord and draw close to your shepherd. It
will deliver you from the spirit of confusion in your ministry.
One day, your shepherd will give you a glimpse of how he
overcame the very problem that you have today. You will be
encouraged by the fact that your shepherd had the same problem
that you now have. You will receive light and wisdom on how to
overcome today.

Chapter 16

Why Sheep Get Sick

1. Sheep get sick because they do not receive the lordship (ownership) of their shepherd.

The statement, "The Lord is my shepherd" is a deep revelation of how a shepherd actually owns the sheep. The lordship of a shepherd reveals the absolute ownership that the shepherd has over the sheep. Because of this powerful ownership, he is able to lead, guide and restore his sheep. He delivers many benefits to the sheep because they are his very own property.

On every farm and in every country, every single sheep or cow actually belongs to someone. That person is the owner and chief shepherd of the sheep.

The Lord is my (*owner*) shepherd; I shall not want. He maketh me to lie down in green pastures: he LEADETH me beside the still waters.

He RESTORETH MY SOUL: he leadeth me (*guidance*) in the paths of righteousness for his name's sake. Yea, though I walk through the valley of the shadow of death, I will FEAR NO EVIL (*discouragement*): for thou art with me; thy rod and thy staff they COMFORT me.

Thou PREPAREST A TABLE before me in the presence of mine enemies: thou ANOINTEST my head with oil; my cup runneth over (*abundant provision*). Surely goodness and mercy shall follow me all the days of my life: and I will dwell in the house of the Lord (my shepherd) FOR EVER (*permanence*).

Psalm 23

Unfortunately, some sheep do not receive the lordship of the shepherd over their lives. This cuts them off from the power and love of the shepherd. They inadvertently "shoot themselves in the foot" by disconnecting themselves from their powerful protector. In the ministry, people who cut themselves from their shepherd simply wither and fade into obscurity.

How to Know When a Sheep Does Not Receive the Lordship of His Shepherd

a. Sheep who do not listen to their pastor's messages are not receiving the lordship of their shepherd.

b. Sheep who do not read the books written by their pastors are not receiving the lordship of their shepherd. They are no more blessed by these materials. They know it all and therefore are not under the lordship of their shepherd.

c. Sheep who do not honour their pastors according to Galatians 6:6 are denying the lordship of their shepherds over them. Why should they honour someone who they do not consider to be their teacher or leader?

d. Sheep declare their independence of their shepherd by not attending important gatherings and meetings. Failure to attend meetings is a declaration by the sheep that, "I am as great as you are and I do not need to come to your meeting." "Verily, verily, I say unto you, The servant is not greater than his lord; neither he that is sent greater than he that sent him" (John 13:16).

2. **Sheep get sick because they do not feed from their shepherd. Shepherds get sick because they do not receive from their chief shepherd.**

   He saith to him again the second time Simon, son of Jonas, lovest thou me? He saith unto him, Yea, Lord; thou knowest that I love thee. He saith unto him, Feed my sheep.

   John 21:16

3. **Sheep get sick because they do not continually receive knowledge and understanding from their shepherd.**

And I will give you pastors according to mine heart, which shall feed you with knowledge and understanding.

Jeremiah 3:15

4. **Sheep get sick because they do not follow their own shepherd. Many of these people follow a thousand different people but do not have a particular shepherd to follow.**

I write not these things to shame you, but as my beloved sons I warn you. For though ye have ten thousand instructors in Christ, yet have ye not many fathers: for in Christ Jesus I HAVE BEGOTTEN YOU through the gospel. Wherefore I beseech you, BE YE FOLLOWERS OF ME.

1 Corinthians 4:1-16

Section 2

THE SHEPHERD

Chapter 17

Three Goals of a Shepherd

1. Every shepherd must desire to become a GOOD shepherd.

I am the good shepherd: the GOOD SHEPHERD giveth his life for the sheep.

John 10:11

a. You are a *good shepherd* when your shepherding style is like that of Christ.

b. You are a *good shepherd* when your pastoring style is like Christ's and your fruits are the same as His.

2. Every shepherd must desire to become a GREAT shepherd.

Now the God of peace, that brought again from the dead our Lord Jesus, that GREAT SHEPHERD of the sheep, through the blood of the everlasting covenant,

Hebrews 13:20

a. You are a *great shepherd* when you have gained much knowledge and skill as a shepherd.

b. You are a *great shepherd* when you have large numbers of sheep under your care.

c. You are a *great shepherd* when you have pastored successfully for many years.

3. Every shepherd must desire to become a CHIEF shepherd.

And when the CHIEF SHEPHERD shall appear, ye shall receive a crown of glory that fadeth not away.

1 Peter 5:4

a. You become a *chief shepherd* when you have other under-shepherds under you. Being a chief shepherd is the same as being an overseer of other pastors.

Chapter 18

How to Identify Shepherds Who Do Not Enter by the Door

Verily, verily, I say unto you, He that ENTERETH
NOT BY THE DOOR into the sheepfold, but climbeth
up some other way, the same is a thief and a robber.

John 10:1

1. **Entrance to ministry must be through the call of God. The door to ministry is the call of God.**

   And no man taketh this honour unto himself, but HE
   THAT IS CALLED OF GOD, as was Aaron.

   Hebrews 5:4

If you do not have a divine call, you are not supposed to be in the ministry. You must have a personal conviction of a call which sets you apart for the ministry.

Your call to ministry is the foundation of your ministry. It defines everything that you will ever do in the ministry.

2. **The door to ministry is different from the door to other professions.**

Your entrance to the medical profession is by graduating from a medical school. The entrance to the legal profession is by graduating from a law school. The entrance to the accounting profession is by obtaining an accountancy certificate. However, the entrance to ministry *is not* by acquiring a certificate from any school, including a Bible school. The entrance to ministry is by receiving and obeying a divine call.

3. **People who do not enter into the ministry through a call have the same effect on the ministry as thieves and robbers.**

Verily, verily, I say unto you, He that ENTERETH NOT BY THE DOOR into the sheepfold, but climbeth up some other way, the same is a thief and a robber.

John 10:1

Imagine having a host of people who are not medical doctors but pose as medical doctors. Imagine having unqualified pharmacists dispensing wrong drugs to innocent people. You would not be wrong to call these people thieves, robbers or murderers. Imagine having someone to be your president who did not really win the election. Everyone would call him a thief and a robber and that is what he is because he "stole" the election.

As soon as someone tries to be a minister without having a genuine call, he is like a thief and a robber. He has taken up a position that does not belong to him and that is what makes him a thief. It is the presence of such people in the ministry that generates so much confusion for onlookers. It is possible that a large percentage of people who are Reverend Ministers were never called into the ministry. Indeed, true shepherds, genuine pastors, thieves and robbers stand side by side in ministry wearing the same clerical collars. Mercy!

4. Identify people who enter the ministry because they are prominent in secular society.

The fact that you are an important person in society does not mean that you must be important in the church. Your secular importance does not mean that you can exercise authority or leadership in a church setting. Also, the fact that your parents were pastors does not mean that you have authority in the church. Leadership in the church is by having the call of God.

Now Korah, the son of Izhar, the son of Kohath, the son of Levi, and Dathan and Abiram, the sons of Eliab, and On, the son of Peleth, sons of Reuben, took men:

And they rose up before Moses, with certain of the children of Israel, two hundred and fifty princes of

the assembly, FAMOUS IN THE CONGREGATION, MEN OF RENOWN:

And they gathered themselves together against Moses and against Aaron, and said unto them, Ye take too much upon you, seeing all the congregation are holy, every one of them, and the LORD is among them: wherefore then lift ye up yourselves above the congregation of the LORD?

Numbers 16:1-3

5. Identify people who enter the ministry because they are urged on by the people.

Saul came on the scene because the people wanted a king. You must not come into ministry because people want you to. You must come into the ministry because God has called you. The voice of the people is *not* the voice of God! The voice of the majority is *not* the voice of God! Don't make the mistake of transposing secular values into the church world.

And said unto him, Behold, thou art old, and thy sons walk not in thy ways: now make us a king to judge us like all the nations. But the thing displeased Samuel, when they said, Give us a king to judge us. And Samuel prayed unto the LORD. And the LORD said unto Samuel, Hearken unto THE VOICE OF THE PEOPLE in all that they say unto thee: for they have not rejected thee, but they have rejected me, that I should not reign over them.

1 Samuel 8:5-7

6. Identify people who enter the ministry through a popular uprising.

Such people gain their authority by challenging and questioning the existing leadership. They question everything that is done and throw doubt and suspicion into the air.

Now Korah, the son of Izhar, the son of Kohath, the son of Levi, and Dathan and Abiram, the sons of Eliab, and On, the son of Peleth, sons of Reuben, took men:

And they rose up before Moses, with certain of the children of Israel, two hundred and fifty princes of the assembly, famous in the congregation, men of renown:

And THEY GATHERED THEMSELVES TOGETHER AGAINST MOSES and against Aaron, and said unto them, Ye take too much upon you, seeing all the congregation are holy, every one of them, and the LORD is among them: wherefore then lift ye up yourselves above the congregation of the LORD?

Numbers 16:1-3

Many pastors enter the ministry through rebellion. After a popular uprising against the existing leadership, a pastor usually emerges and begins his own ministry. Such people are like Korah who were birthed into public ministry by fighting existing leadership. These people have no foundation in the ministry and are doomed to fail. Their end will be like the end of Korah! Eventually, they will be destroyed! They will not be able to maintain their position of leadership because they came into ministry the wrong way. Fighting existing leadership is the wrong way into the ministry.

I have watched as some pastors have woven their way into ministry by fighting me. They have criticised me and poisoned the minds of innocent members against my leadership. Through this kind of propaganda, they created a following and started their own ministries. But what can a man accomplish if he has no foundation? It is only a fool who builds his house on the sand of criticism, backbiting and slander! You must build your house on the rock. The rock is the Word of God! The rock is the call of God! All those who build their house on the sand will live to see their houses collapse on their very heads.

7. **Identify people who enter the ministry not appreciating the great privilege given to them to serve in the house of the Lord.**

These people are presumptuous and take for granted existing leadership and authority structures. They move out of rank, speaking about things that do not concern them. Presumption is defined as "the arrogant assumption of privilege!" People are presumptuous when they feel that the call of God is no "big deal" and it is not such a special thing to be a pastor. Such people do not see any barriers between themselves and the leadership of the church. *They say in their hearts "I can be you", "I can do what you are doing".* Such people want to be Reverend ministers and declare their equality with all other Reverend ministers. This is presumption and is a dangerous trait that causes people to erroneously move into things they are not called to.

> **And Moses said unto Korah, Hear, I pray you, ye sons of Levi: SEEMETH IT BUT A SMALL THING UNTO YOU, THAT THE GOD OF ISRAEL HATH SEPARATED YOU FROM THE CONGREGATION OF ISRAEL, to bring you near to himself to do the service of the tabernacle of the LORD, and to stand before the congregation to minister unto them? And he hath brought thee near to him, and all thy brethren the sons of Levi with thee: and seek ye the priesthood also?**
> **Numbers 16:8-10**

8. Identify people who enter the ministry relying on the sentiments created by murmuring in the congregation.

Immature and inexperienced people gain confidence through murmuring. They feel because a lot of people murmur, there must be something right about it. It does sound right and it does generate feelings of self-righteousness but it is still wrong. Do not allow undertone discussions and generalized murmuring to give you false confidence about anything.

The Word of God and the call of God stand alone as the reason why you should do things. The Word of God is a rock. The murmuring of the people is sand. Do not build your house on the sand. Build your house on the rock!

> **Now Korah, the son of Izhar, the son of Kohath, the son of Levi, and Dathan and Abiram, the sons of Eliab, and On, the son of Peleth, sons of Reuben, TOOK**

MEN: AND THEY ROSE UP BEFORE MOSES, with certain of the children of Israel, two hundred and fifty princes of the assembly, famous in the congregation, men of renown: And they gathered themselves together against Moses and against Aaron ...

Numbers 16:1-3a

9. **Identify people who enter ministry relying on the reputation and prominence of rebellious people they have recruited.**

Unfortunately people are impressed with outward appearances of wealth and authority. They think that pomposity and human importance gives enough weight for ministry work. Big shot behaviour, expensive cars, throwing money around and throwing your weight around is no substitute for the call of God!

Rebellious people who are fatally deficient in God's grace, depend on such things to boost their confidence as they tread into waters they have no business going into.

Now Korah, the son of Izhar, the son of Kohath, the son of Levi, and Dathan and Abiram, the sons of Eliab, and On, the son of Peleth, sons of Reuben, took men:

And they rose up before Moses, with certain of the children of Israel, two hundred and fifty princes of the assembly, FAMOUS IN THE CONGREGATION, MEN OF RENOWN:

And they gathered themselves together against Moses and against Aaron ...

Numbers 16:1-3a

10. **Identify people who enter the ministry and prophecy even though they have not been sent.**

Some people enter the ministry because they have no other options. God did not speak to them, yet they ran! God did not send them, yet they went! They see the ministry as a good career option!

I once heard a minister on television saying that he came into the ministry because he was not good at chemistry, history, maths, biology or any of the other subjects. That is why he entered into the ministry. Is it not amazing that people can shamelessly fulfil such Scriptures on television for us all to see? They were not sent but they went! They were not spoken to by God but they began to prophesy and to teach!

Learn to identify such people and do not sit under their ministries because you will be sitting under the wrong person!

I have not sent these prophets, yet they ran: I have not spoken to them, yet they prophesied.

Jeremiah 23:21

11. Identify people who enter the ministry through false dreams.

Many people have false dreams. Unfortunately, some actually enter the ministry because of a false dream. As you can see, false ministry will not really benefit the people. The Lord has cursed false prophets because they cause the people to err through their lives. Almost every minister claims to have heard from the Lord before embarking on his mission. Unfortunately, some saw visions and dreams of their own hearts. All these ministries must be left to time. We shall know them by their fruits.

Behold, I am against them that PROPHESY FALSE DREAMS, saith the LORD, and do tell them, AND CAUSE MY PEOPLE TO ERR BY THEIR LIES, and by their lightness; yet I sent them not, nor commanded them: therefore they shall not profit this people at all, saith the LORD.

Jeremiah 23:32

12. Identify people who enter the ministry casually, not considering the gravity of what it means to work for God.

This is what Jeremiah meant when he said the people use lightness to minister. The ministry is no easy job.

One day, somebody saw me driving a nice car and I heard him make an amazing comment. He said, "We should all become pastors and start churches, then we will have such nice cars." God made me hear the voice of that ignoramus because it is the secret thought of many other ignoramuses. I welcome anyone who wants to become a minister so that he can have a nice car but I would advise him to take some bandages for his wounds, for when he falls flat on his face!

The ministry is no easy job and no one should venture into ministry using lightness. I often recognize wisdom in people who hesitate to come into full-time ministry. I often sense caution and carefulness in them and I know they are wisely considering the realities of what ministry entails. Anyone who lightly takes on the job of ministry does not understand what he is doing.

Behold, I am against them that prophesy false dreams, saith the LORD, and do tell them, and cause my people to err by their lies, AND BY THEIR LIGHTNESS; YET I SENT THEM NOT, nor commanded them: therefore they shall not profit this people at all, saith the LORD.

Jeremiah 23:32

13. Identify people who enter the ministry through lies and deception.

Some people even enter into ministry through lies and deception. They claim to have a call but they do not have one. Some need a job and instead of just saying so, they launch into a spiritual discourse about having a call. Many of these are simply lies and hypocrisy. Such people jump out of ministry when they have an opportunity and it becomes evident that they were lying all along about their call to ministry.

For I have not sent them, saith the LORD, yet THEY PROPHESY A LIE IN MY NAME; that I might drive you out, and that ye might perish, ye, and the prophets that prophesy unto you.

Jeremiah 27:15

14. Identify people who enter the ministry because they have an unusual ability to make people believe and trust things that are not true.

False prophets criticise and accuse existing leaders. They make the masses trust in things that are not true. They make them suspect their existing leaders of evil. Jeremiah was seen as an evil person predicting destruction on Jerusalem because the false prophet Hananiah was lying to them. The character of Satan is to lie and to deceive the whole world. Satan's lying ministers also cleverly deceive large groups of people into believing things that are not true.

> **Then said the prophet Jeremiah unto Hananiah the prophet, Hear now, Hananiah; The LORD hath not sent thee; but THOU MAKEST THIS PEOPLE TO TRUST IN A LIE.**
>
> **Jeremiah 28:15**

> **Send to all them of the captivity, saying, Thus saith the LORD concerning Shemaiah the Nehelamite; Because that Shemaiah hath prophesied unto you, and I sent him not, and he caused you to trust in a lie:**
>
> **Jeremiah 29:31**

Many large and popular ministries are preaching doctrines which are not the main stream Gospel. They sound like the Gospel, but it is not the Gospel. God is not pleased with them and God is not pleased with their messages because it is not the Gospel He sent us to preach.

But the money-loving carnal masses lap it all up gleefully and tell the pastor that they have never heard such wonderful messages before! Large scale deception is therefore delivered to God's people through false prophets. These modern false prophets look like twenty-first century "ne'er do wrong" angels, who are perfect examples of success and wealth and who know all the steps to life and the reasons for everything in this world.

But like Job's three friends, these pastors who seem to know the reasons for everything that is happening in your life are actually wrong about many things. In the end, Job was the righteous one and Jobs' friends were declared to be sinners. Many of these pastors will be declared to sinners on the Judgement day.

15. Identify people who enter ministry through the powers of darkness.

I once preached in a small church which had unusual doctrines. When I did the altar call, all the pastors gave their lives to Christ. Even the senior pastor gave his life to Jesus Christ. One may ask how such people became pastors and by what spirit they were operating. There are definitely false churches with false prophets who came into the ministry through divination and vanity. How can you know the difference between a false minister and a real minister? I can't really tell but sometimes you see a minister that your heart is not drawn to. Often, God is not drawing you to that ministry.

There is often no way to tell whether it is right or wrong. Since you cannot see into the hearts of men, you must be careful not to comment. Just rely on your heart and whether you are drawn to it or not.

Remember the Scripture that teaches us not to judge from the outward appearance. There will always be ministries which look like false ministries but are actually genuine. Remember that every tree that the Father has not planted will be uprooted!

They have seen vanity AND LYING DIVINATION, saying, The LORD saith: and the LORD hath not sent them: and they have made others to hope that they would confirm the word.

Ezekiel 13:6

Chapter 19

The Shepherding Assignments: To Be Gentle and Tender

Five Reasons to be Gentle and Tender

1. Shepherds must be gentle and tender because the children are tender.

   And he said unto him, My lord knoweth that THE CHILDREN ARE TENDER, and the flocks and herds with young are with me: and if men should overdrive them one day, all the flock will die.

   Genesis 33:13

2. Shepherds must be gentle and tender because there are young ones among the flocks and the herds.

   And he said unto him, My lord knoweth that the children are tender, and THE FLOCKS AND HERDS WITH YOUNG ARE WITH ME: and if men should overdrive them one day, all the flock will die.

   Genesis 33:13

3. Shepherds must be gentle and tender because your flocks will die if you overdrive them.

   And he said unto him, My lord knoweth that the children are tender, and the flocks and herds with young are with me: and IF MEN SHOULD OVERDRIVE THEM ONE DAY, ALL THE FLOCK WILL DIE.

   Genesis 33:13

4. Shepherds must be gentle and tender because flocks must be led softly.

   Let my lord, I pray thee, pass over before his servant: and I will LEAD ON SOFTLY, according as the cattle

that goeth before me and the children be able to endure, until I come unto my lord unto Seir.

Genesis 33:14

5. Shepherds must be gentle and tender because the flock can only be led as much as the children can endure.

Let my lord, I pray thee, pass over before his servant: and I will lead on softly, ACCORDING AS the cattle that goeth before me and THE CHILDREN BE ABLE TO ENDURE, until I come unto my lord unto Seir.

Genesis 33:14

Chapter 20

The Shepherding Assignments:
To Guide and to Lead

1. A shepherd must lead his sheep by still waters.

He maketh me to lie down in green pastures: he LEADETH ME BESIDE THE STILL WATERS.

Psalms 23:2

2. A shepherd must lead his sheep to green pastures.

He maketh me to lie down in green pastures...

Psalms 23:2

3. A shepherd must guide his sheep through wilderness situations.

But made his own people to go forth like sheep, and GUIDED THEM IN THE WILDERNESS LIKE A FLOCK. And he led them on safely, so that they feared not: but the sea overwhelmed their enemies. And he brought them to the border of his sanctuary, even to this mountain, which his right hand had purchased.

Psalms 78:52-54

4. A shepherd must lead his people like a flock.

To lead the people like a flock speaks of learning the principles of leading large numbers of people with diverse opinions, backgrounds and beliefs. The art of shepherding is the art of leading people in spite of opposition from independent sheep, opinion leaders and rebellious people. It is also the art of leading people who are so many that you cannot talk to each one personally.

Thou leddest thy people like a flock by the hand of Moses and Aaron.

Psalm 77:20

Chapter 21

The Shepherding Assignments: To Watch for the Sheep

Five Ways a Shepherd Must Watch for the Sheep

1. *Shepherds must watch out for the soul, mind and the heart of the sheep.* Perhaps it is by being a farmer that you would understand the need to watch out for the innermost workings of the sheep God has given you. Being a shepherd is the same as being a farmer.

A farmer once told me of how he spent his savings to purchase some day-old chicks for his chicken farm.

He said to me, "After I purchased these day-old chicks I fed them earnestly and watched for them to grow, but they failed to grow."

He told me, "I tried everything I could. I got the vet to come. I gave them extra food. I gave them vitamins. I spent so much money on these chickens but they simply did not grow!"

What this poor farmer did not know was that there was something inherently wrong with the chicks. He had purchased chicks that did not have the ability to grow. The chickens had a problem with their "soul". They were "abnormal chicks" who lacked the normal ability to grow.

Another farmer told me how his pigs simply did not grow in spite of all that he did to make them grow.

These farming problems are the reasons why a shepherd must constantly watch out for the soul, mind and heart of the sheep. He is looking to see if there is something wrong deep inside. It is the deep inner problems of the sheep that prevent them from growing.

Obey them that have the rule over you, and submit yourselves: for THEY WATCH FOR YOUR SOULS, as they that must give account, that they may do it with joy, and not with grief: for that is unprofitable for you.

Hebrews 13:17

2. *Shepherds must watch for the very lives of their sheep.* Satan also wishes to kill your members. It is the duty of the pastor to pray for the preservation of the life of the sheep. God will spare their lives because of your prayers.

Take heed therefore unto yourselves, and to all the flock, over the which the Holy Ghost hath made you overseers, to feed the church of God, which he hath purchased with his own blood. For I know this, that after my departing shall grievous wolves enter in among you, not sparing the flock. Also of your own selves shall men arise, speaking perverse things, to draw away disciples after them. Therefore watch, and remember, that by the space of three years I ceased not to warn every one night and day with tears.

Acts 20:28-31

3. *Shepherds must watch for the souls of the sheep by being constantly in prayer and thanksgiving.*

Continue in prayer, and watch in the same with thanksgiving;

Colossians 4:2

4. *Shepherds must watch for the souls of the sheep by praying in the night for them.* Praying at night is called "watching and praying." Jesus commanded us to watch and pray. Watching and praying speaks of waiting on God in the night time.

Therefore let us not sleep, as do others; but let us watch and be sober.

1 Thessalonians 5:6

5. *Shepherds must watch for the souls of the sheep by watching out for the enemy.* There is always an enemy trying to steal our sheep. I remember a brother who reared chickens. One night, a cat came into the chicken coop and killed several of the chickens. The cat obviously could not eat more than one chicken but ended up killing more than fifty of them. This is the wickedness of the enemy who comes to destroy the work that we are doing. By the time the devil has finished going through the congregation, people are senselessly destroyed and are unable to be a part of a church anymore.

But watch thou in all things, endure afflictions, do the work of an evangelist, make full proof of thy ministry.
2 Timothy 4:5

Chapter 22

Jehovah the
Protecting Shepherd

The Protection of a Shepherd

1. *Like Jehovah the great shepherd, pastors must protect their sheep by defending them against attacks.* God defends His sheep through the shepherds. Jehovah, the good shepherd, defends His sheep.

My defence is of God, which saveth the upright in heart.

Psalms 7:10

But I will sing of thy power; yea, I will sing aloud of thy mercy in the morning: for thou hast been my defence and refuge in the day of my trouble.

Psalms 59:16

He only is my rock and my salvation: he is my defence; I shall not be moved.

Psalms 62:6

The LORD of hosts shall defend them; and they shall devour, and subdue with sling stones; and they shall drink, and make a noise as through wine; and they shall be filled like bowls, and as the corners of the altar.

Zechariah 9:15

2. *Like Jehovah the great shepherd, pastors must protect their sheep by being keepers of the sheep.* Shepherds stabilize the life of their sheep. Jehovah, the great shepherd, is also the keeper of the sheep. He stabilizes their life and their feet shall not be moved.

He will not suffer thy foot to be moved: he that keepeth thee will not slumber.

Psalm 121:3

3. *Like Jehovah the great shepherd, pastors must protect the sheep from the influence of this modern godless generation.* Jehovah, the good shepherd, protects the sheep from the influence of this generation. Shepherds protect their sheep from the influence of their generation.

Thou shalt keep them, O LORD, thou shalt preserve them from this generation for ever.

Psalm 12:7

4. *Like Jehovah the great shepherd, pastors must protect the sheep from pride.* Jehovah, the good shepherd, protects His sheep from pride. Shepherds can protect their sheep from pride by preaching and teaching about humility and the nothingness of man in relation to God.

Thou shalt hide them in the secret of thy presence from the pride of man: thou shalt keep them secretly in a pavilion from the strife of tongues.

Psalm 31:20

5. *Like Jehovah the great shepherd, pastors must protect the sheep by being available to the sheep.* The sheep must know where to always find the shepherd. Jehovah, the reliable shepherd, can be counted on and can be found by looking to the hills. Shepherds are reliable; their sheep can count on them.

I will lift up mine eyes unto the hills, from whence cometh my help. My help cometh from the LORD, which made heaven and earth. He will not suffer thy foot to be moved: HE THAT KEEPETH THEE WILL NOT SLUMBER.

Psalm 121:1-3

6. *Like Jehovah the great shepherd, pastors must protect their sheep by committing them to God.* Jesus committed all His sheep to Jehovah for keeping. Shepherds must follow the example of Christ and commit their sheep to God.

And now I am no more in the world, but these are in the world, and I come to thee. HOLY FATHER, KEEP THROUGH THINE OWN NAME THOSE whom thou hast given me, that they may be one, as we are.

John 17:11

Chapter 23

The Shepherding Assignments: To Feed

1. *The shepherd must make the sheep lie down in green pastures and prepare a table for them to feed them.* The green pastures and still waters help relax the sheep and this enables them to feed.

> **The LORD is my shepherd; I shall not want. He maketh me to lie down in green pastures: he leadeth me beside the still waters. He restoreth my soul: he leadeth me in the paths of righteousness for his name's sake. Yea, though I walk through the valley of the shadow of death, I will fear no evil: for thou art with me; thy rod and thy staff they comfort me. Thou preparest a table before me in the presence of mine enemies: thou anointest my head with oil; my cup runneth over. Surely goodness and mercy shall follow me all the days of my life: and I will dwell in the house of the LORD for ever.**
>
> **Psalm 23**

2. *The shepherd must gather the sheep, carry them and gently lead them to the place where he can feed them.* If you do not have the time or heart to gather the people you are leading and gently carry them along, you will never have the chance to feed them. Without this kind of gentleness, the sheep will not be open to receive from the shepherd.

> **He shall feed his flock like a shepherd: he shall gather the lambs with his arm, and carry them in his bosom, and shall gently lead those that are with young.**
>
> **Isaiah 40:11**

3. *The shepherd must feed the sheep with knowledge and understanding.* The knowledge of God, the fear of God and spiritual understanding will greatly transform the lives of your

members. The shepherd must avoid administering material that should be taught in secular schools and universities. Those things have their place, but we must be teachers of the Word of God.

And I will give you pastors according to mine heart, which shall feed you with knowledge and understanding.

Jeremiah 3:15

Chapter 24

The Shepherding Assignments:
To Restore and to Heal

1. *Shepherds must be valuable physicians to the sheep.* Through shepherds, healing must come to the bodies of the sick.

   But ye are forgers of lies, ye are all PHYSICIANS OF NO VALUE.

   Job 13:4

2. *Shepherds are also to heal the brokenhearted, bound, poor, blind and hurting people.*

   The Spirit of the Lord is upon me, because he hath anointed me to preach the gospel to the poor; he hath sent me to heal the brokenhearted, to preach deliverance to the captives, and recovering of sight to the blind, to set at liberty them that are bruised,

   Luke 4:18

3. *Shepherds must help people who are not well, people who are not complete and people who are not whole.*

   But when Jesus heard that, he said unto them, They that be whole need not a physician, but they that are sick.

   Matthew 9:12

4. *Shepherds must restore the mind, the heart, and the emotions of the sheep.* That is what is meant by restoring the soul.

   He restoreth my soul: he leadeth me in the paths of righteousness for his name's sake.

   Psalms 23:3

5. *Shepherds must help people to recover what they have lost through their own sin and rebellion.*

And the king answered and said unto the man of God, Intreat now the face of the LORD thy God, and pray for me, that my hand may be restored me again. And the man of God besought the LORD, and the king's hand was restored him again, and became as it was before.

1 Kings 13:6

6. *Shepherds must restore life and normalcy to the sheep.*

Then spake Elisha unto THE WOMAN, WHOSE SON HE HAD RESTORED TO LIFE, saying, Arise, and go thou and thine household, and sojourn wheresoever thou canst sojourn: for the LORD hath called for a famine; and it shall also come upon the land seven years.

2 Kings 8:1

After that he put his hands again upon his eyes, and made him look up: and HE WAS RESTORED, AND SAW EVERY MAN CLEARLY.

Mark 8:25

And looking round about upon them all, he said unto the man, Stretch forth thy hand. And he did so: and HIS HAND WAS RESTORED WHOLE as the other.

Luke 6:10

Chapter 25

Vampire Pastors

What is a vampire? It is a creature that drinks your blood. It lives by sucking your very life away. A vampire does not give you anything for sucking your blood. It simply takes away your life and your blood.

Unfortunately, some shepherds simply take away from the life of the sheep. Most definitely, a shepherd will benefit from the sheep he has reared. He will have a day when he will enjoy things that are brought to him by his sheep. That is not what I am talking about.

A real pastor loves his sheep and gives his life for them. A pastor without a servant's heart will only take away from the sheep.

Contrast this with, a good shepherd who lays down his very life for the sheep. A good shepherd gives many things to his sheep. A good shepherd does many things for his sheep. Are you a giver or a taker? A giver is a real shepherd. If all you do is to take away from the people you oversee, then you are a vampire.

Many secular leaders are also vampires. They take away the wealth of the nation and live in palaces whilst the millions under their leadership live in squalor and poverty. It is easy to recognize a nation that has been led by vampires. Just take a look around and you will see how the kings that have ruled took away the lives and wealth of the masses.

When Israel wanted a king the Lord showed them what it would mean for them to have a king. This king would take away many things from them. He would be their leader, but *he would basically take away from them.* God was trying to warn them of the coming of the vampires. When you become a shepherd, are you going to be a "vampire pastor" and take away from the life of the sheep? Are you going to be like Jesus and give your very life for the sheep?

1. **A vampire shepherd will take your children and make them his servants.** Instead of investing in your children and making them grow up to be better people, he will take advantage of them. The vampire pastor will take the children for himself. What can you give to the children that God sends to you?

   And Samuel told all the words of the LORD unto the people that asked of him a king. And he said, This will be the manner of the king that shall reign over you: HE WILL TAKE your sons, and appoint them for himself, for his chariots, and to be his horsemen; and some shall run before his chariots.

   1 Samuel 8:10-11

2. **A vampire pastor will take your sons until you cry.** What can you do for the sons? Do you just take away from them or will you invest in them? A vampire pastor does not recognize the importance of the young ones. He does not see the future that they hold. He does not recognize that they will become the next generation of leaders.

   And Samuel told all the words of the Lord unto the people that asked of him a king. And he said, this will be the manner of the king that shall reign over you: He will take your sons, and appoint them for himself, for his chariots, and to be his horsemen; and some shall run before his chariots.... And ye shall cry out in that day because of your king which ye shall have chosen you; and the Lord will not hear you in that day.

   1 Samuel 8:10-11, 18

3. **A vampire pastor will take away your daughters and mistreat them.** What can you do for the daughters? Do you just take away from them or will you invest in them? A vampire pastor will see all the young ladies in the church as people he can take advantage of. Do you not see the potential in the daughters? They will become lady pastors and singers in the future. They will make you glad one day.

And HE WILL TAKE your daughters to be confectionaries, and to be cooks, and to be bakers.

1 Samuel 8:13

4. **A vampire pastor will just take away your fields until you cry.** What can you do about the fields and businesses of your members? Can you help them to get richer? Can you arrange for them to have any business contacts? Can you give anything to them to help them? Or do you just take away from them? A real pastor will urge his members on until their fields and houses are multiplied.

And HE WILL TAKE your fields, and your vineyards, and your oliveyards, even the best of them, and give them to his servants.

1 Samuel 8:14

5. **A vampire pastor will take away a tenth of your seed and your vineyards until you cry.** A vampire pastor will take away the tithe and make you cry. You will never see or understand what the tithe has been used for. A good pastor will take the tithe but you will be glad that he has received it because it will be used for the right thing and will benefit the congregation at the end of the day.

And HE WILL TAKE the tenth of your seed, and of your vineyards, and give to his officers, and to his servants.

1 Samuel 8:15

6. **A vampire pastor will take your servants and your animals until you cry.** Vampire pastors spy the possessions of their members with covetous eyes! They desire the privileges and wealth of the richest members. Dear pastor, do you have the eyes of a vampire hoping that your members hand over their hard-earned possessions to you?

And HE WILL TAKE your menservants, and your maidservants, and your goodliest young men, and your asses, and put them to his work.

1 Samuel 8:16

7. **A vampire pastor will take the tenth of your sheep until you cry.** Do you take offerings from your congregations until they cry, "Enough! Enough! We can not give anymore!" Do you give anything back to the sheep? Do you take so much from the members until they are impoverished by your kind of leadership?

African countries have been impoverished through heads of state who have shown this kind of "take, take, take" mentality. Their "take away" leadership style has turned Africa into a barren land of scarcity and tribal warfare.

HE WILL TAKE the tenth of your sheep: and ye shall be his servants.

And YE SHALL CRY out in that day because of your king which ye shall have chosen you; and the LORD will not hear you in that day.

Nevertheless the people refused to obey the voice of Samuel; and they said, Nay; but we will have a king over us;

That we also may be like all the nations; and that our king may judge us, and go out before us, and fight our battles.

And Samuel heard all the words of the people, and he rehearsed them in the ears of the LORD.

1 Samuel 8:17-21

Three Types of Servant-Pastors

Pastors must not lord it over the sheep but must strive to be servants of the people whom God has called us to. The pompous attitude of many leaders is unfortunately quite different from what Christ taught. Let us turn our attention now to another kind shepherd: the servant-shepherd. There are three types of servant-shepherds. Pastors with a servant's heart will give rather than take from the people. I have identified three kinds of servant-pastors.

1. *Diakoneo* pastors: These are pastors who wait upon someone. *Diakoneo* is a Greek word which speaks of waiting upon another or acting as a host, a friend or a teacher. The first person a diakoneo pastor must *wait upon is the Lord.* God may also give you a ministry in which you have to *wait on someone.* This is a powerful ministry and you must not despise it. Martha was a good example of a *diakoneo* person.

   There they made him a supper; and Martha served: but Lazarus was one of them that sat at the table with him. Then took Mary a pound of ointment of spikenard, very costly, and anointed the feet of Jesus, and wiped his feet with her hair: and the house was filled with the odour of the ointment.

   John 12:2-3

2. *Diakonia* pastors: These people offer assistance or service to someone. *Diakonia* is a Greek word which refers to *giving assistance or service* to someone. Many pastors are called to assist someone. It is disastrous when someone whose calling is to assist is forced to be the head of a church. Many good "leading leaders" are not good assistants and many good assistants are not good "leading leaders". Do not despise the calling of the assistant. It is the call of the servant pastor.

   I know thy works, and charity, AND SERVICE, and faith, and thy patience, and thy works; and the last to be more than the first.

   Revelation 2:19

   Or did I commit a sin in humbling myself so that you might be exalted, because I preached the gospel of God to you without charge?
   I robbed other churches by TAKING WAGES FROM THEM TO SERVE YOU;

   2 Corinthians 11:7-8 (NASB)

3. *Diakonos* pastors: These are pastors who run errands and do menial jobs. *Diakonos* is a Greek word which describes an attendant, a waiter at table or some other menial function.

You must not shy away from any menial jobs. Many menial jobs are actually ministry work. Many times, to despise menial jobs is to despise your very ministry.

All my state shall Tychicus declare unto you, who is a beloved brother, and a faithful minister and fellowservant in the Lord:

Colossian 4:7

Chapter 26

The Shepherding Skills
of Jehovah

I was pleasantly surprised to find that it is not only Jesus who is described as a shepherd. Jehovah also describes Himself as shepherd! All through the Old Testament, Jehovah describes Himself as the shepherd who works hard to take care of His sheep. What better example could we learn from than the example of Jehovah Himself? Let us look at some of the key activities that Almighty God Himself undertakes as He demonstrates the true functions of a shepherd.

Fifteen Ways Jehovah Demonstrates Shepherding Skills

1. Jehovah, the greatest shepherd, searches out the lost sheep.

For thus saith the Lord GOD; Behold, I, even I, WILL BOTH SEARCH MY SHEEP, AND SEEK THEM OUT. AS A SHEPHERD seeketh out his flock in the day that he is among his sheep that are scattered; so will I seek out my sheep, and will deliver them out of all places where they have been scattered in the cloudy and dark day. And I will bring them out from the people, and gather them from the countries, and will bring them to their own land, and feed them upon the mountains of Israel by the rivers, and in all the inhabited places of the country.

Ezekiel 34:11-13

2. Jehovah, the greatest shepherd, delivers sheep that have been held captive.

AS A SHEPHERD seeketh out his flock in the day that he is among his sheep that are scattered; so will I seek out my sheep, and WILL DELIVER THEM out of all places where they have been scattered in the cloudy and dark day.

Ezekiel 34:12

3. Jehovah, the greatest shepherd, gathers the dispersed sheep.

AS A SHEPHERD seeketh out his flock in the day that he is among his sheep that are scattered; so will I seek out my sheep, and will deliver them out of all places where they have been scattered in the cloudy and dark day. And I will bring them out from the people, and GATHER THEM from the countries, and will bring them to their own land, and feed them upon the mountains of Israel by the rivers, and in all the inhabited places of the country.

Ezekiel 34:12-13

4. Jehovah, the greatest shepherd, feeds the hungry sheep.

I WILL FEED THEM IN A GOOD PASTURE, and upon the high mountains of Israel shall their fold be: there shall they lie in a good fold, and in a fat pasture shall they feed upon the mountains of Israel. I will feed my flock, and I will cause them to lie down, saith the Lord GOD.

Ezekiel 34:14-15

5. Jehovah, the greatest shepherd, provides rest for the weary sheep.

I will feed them in a good pasture, and upon the high mountains of Israel shall their fold be: THERE SHALL THEY LIE IN A GOOD FOLD, and in a fat pasture shall they feed upon the mountains of Israel. I will feed my flock, and I WILL CAUSE THEM TO LIE DOWN, saith the Lord GOD.

Ezekiel 34:14-15

6. Jehovah, the greatest shepherd, binds up the hurt sheep.

I will seek that which was lost, and bring again that which was driven away, and WILL BIND UP that which was broken, and will strengthen that which was sick: but I will destroy the fat and the strong; I will feed them with judgment.

Ezekiel 34:16

7. Jehovah, the greatest shepherd, strengthens the weak sheep.

I will seek that which was lost, and bring again that which was driven away, and will bind up that which was broken, and will STRENGTHEN THAT WHICH WAS SICK: but I will destroy the fat and the strong; I will feed them with judgment.

Ezekiel 34:16

8. Jehovah, the greatest shepherd, guides the directionless sheep.

For thus saith the Lord God; Behold, I, even I, will both search my sheep, and seek them out.

AS A SHEPHERD seeketh out his flock in the day that he is among his sheep that are scattered; so will I seek out my sheep, and will deliver them out of all places where they have been scattered in the cloudy and dark day.

And I WILL BRING THEM OUT from the people, and gather them from the countries, and will BRING THEM TO THEIR OWN LAND, and feed them upon the mountains of Israel by the rivers, and in all the inhabited places of the country.

Ezekiel 34:11-13

9. Jehovah, the greatest shepherd, carries his broken sheep.

Behold, the Lord God will come with strong hand, and his arm shall rule for him: behold, his reward is with him, and his work before him. He shall feed his flock LIKE A SHEPHERD: he shall gather the lambs with his arm, and CARRY THEM IN HIS BOSOM, and shall gently lead those that are with young.

Isaiah 40: 10-11

10. Jehovah, the greatest shepherd, ensures that the sheep lack nothing.

The LORD is my shepherd; I shall not want.

Psalm 23:1

11. Jehovah, the greatest shepherd, restores the soul of his tired sheep.

THE LORD IS MY SHEPHERD; I shall not want. He maketh me to lie down in green pastures: he leadeth me beside the still waters. HE RESTORETH MY SOUL: he leadeth me in the paths of righteousness for his name's sake.

Psalm 23:1-3

12. Jehovah, the greatest shepherd, leads the sheep in godly ways of righteousness.

He restoreth my soul: he leadeth me in the paths of righteousness for his name's sake.

Psalm 23:3

13. Jehovah, the greatest shepherd, prepares a table for frightened sheep in the presence of enemies.

The LORD is my shepherd; I shall not want...Thou preparest a table before me in the presence of mine enemies: thou anointest my head with oil; my cup runneth over.

Psalm 23:1,5

14. Jehovah, the greatest shepherd, comforts the agitated sheep.

Yea, though I walk through the valley of the shadow of death, I will fear no evil: for thou art with me; thy rod and thy staff they comfort me.

Psalm 23:4

15. Jehovah, the greatest shepherd, anoints his needy sheep.

The LORD is my shepherd; I shall not want...Thou preparest a table before me in the presence of mine enemies: thou anointest my head with oil; my cup runneth over.

Psalm 23:1,5

Chapter 27

Thirty-Five Keys to Becoming a Good Shepherd

I am the good shepherd: the GOOD SHEPHERD giveth his life for the sheep.

John 10:11

1. *Become a good shepherd by following all the examples set by "the good shepherd!"* Jesus was the good shepherd. Any of us desiring to be a good shepherd or a good pastor must learn directly from Him. In this chapter, you will learn the characteristics of the good shepherd Jesus Christ. If you follow His example, you will be a good pastor. Jesus Christ set the highest standards for us. We need no greater example than the one we have in Christ.

I AM THE GOOD SHEPHERD: the good shepherd giveth his life for the sheep.

John 10:11

I AM THE GOOD SHEPHERD, and know my sheep, and am known of mine.

John 10:14

2. *Become a good shepherd by preaching, teaching and healing.*

And JESUS went about all the cities and villages, TEACHING in their synagogues, and PREACHING the gospel of the kingdom, and HEALING every sickness and every disease among the people.

Matt 9:35

3. *Become a good shepherd by relating to the sheep.* Every shepherd must discover the art of relating with other human beings. Influencing human behaviour is one of the most important skills a pastor must develop. Working with human beings is a very complex undertaking. It is more difficult to

learn how to relate with and influence human beings than to do heart surgery. I have found that pastors live and die without learning this very important skill of relating with and influencing other people.

To him the porter openeth; and the sheep hear his voice: and he CALLETH his own sheep BY NAME, and LEADETH THEM OUT.

John 10:3

4. *Become a good shepherd by fighting all who enter the sheepfold as thieves and robbers.* A good shepherd must recognize that there are many people that seek to destroy what he is building. Enemies are part of life. God told David, "sit down till I make your enemies your footstool." David was constantly aware of the fight he was in for. He was aware of the reality of evil. Don't try to be a nice gentleman, who lives at peace with all and sundry. Sometimes, to be a good shepherd you must label the enemy and fight with him.

Verily, verily, I say unto you, He that ENTERETH NOT BY THE DOOR into the sheepfold, but climbeth up some other way, the same is a thief and a robber.

John 10:1

5. *Become a good shepherd by recognizing and condemning all who have ever tried to take away the sheep.* A good shepherd must teach against the false religions and false shepherds that try to influence them. A good shepherd must openly describe thieves and robbers as Jesus did. Jesus taught that those who came before Him were thieves and robbers. Teach your sheep how to recognize thieves and robbers.

All that ever came before me ARE THIEVES AND ROBBERS: but the sheep did not hear them.

John 10:8

6. *Become a good shepherd by providing a sheepfold for the sheep.* A good shepherd creates a safe home for the sheep. This secure dwelling for a sheep is called a sheepfold. A good shepherd builds church buildings so that his sheep can be

safely nurtured within its four walls. Every good shepherd must try to build something for the sheep.

Verily, verily, I say unto you, He that entereth not by the door INTO THE SHEEPFOLD, but climbeth up some other way, the same is a thief and a robber.

John 10:1

7. *Become a good shepherd by becoming a good leader.* I wrote a book specially for pastors and shepherds called, "The Art of Leadership" I believe one of the most important things that makes you a good shepherd is your ability to be a strong, efficient leader. Leadership must be learned and studied by all pastors. Leadership is a scientific subject that can be learned. The understanding of leadership is the one thing that will transform you from being a shepherd of twenty people into a shepherd of a thousand.

To him the porter openeth; and the sheep hear his voice: and he calleth his own sheep by name, AND LEADETH THEM out.And when he putteth forth his own sheep, he goeth before them, and the sheep follow him: for they know his voice.

John 10:3-4

8. *Become a good shepherd by entering the sheepfold through the right door.* You cannot become a successful shepherd unless you have entered the sheepfold legally. Many shepherds attained their positions illegally. Some stole sheep from other churches, while others destroyed churches in order to build their ministries. Some shepherds have caused the devastation of the churches they used to belong to. Some were assistant pastors and broke away with sections of the congregation. They have used these stolen waters to build their lives and ministries. But a good shepherd starts his ministry (enters the sheepfold) in the right way. The beginning is everything! Beginnings are very important! Foundations determine how far you can go and how much you can do. "If the foundations be destroyed, what can the righteous do?" (Psalm 11:3).

But HE THAT ENTERETH IN BY THE DOOR is the shepherd of the sheep.

John 10:2

9. *Become a good shepherd by having the porter open to you.* To be a good shepherd, you will need to have good relations with the porter. A good shepherd relates with many other people. There are people who only relate with the most senior leader but have no good relationships with other leaders. A good shepherd recognizes that he will need the complementary help of others to accomplish his vision. The porter must open the door for the shepherd to enter the sheepfold and begin his ministry. I have learnt that the success of almost every minister is greatly dependent on the help he receives.

But he that entereth in by the door is the shepherd of the sheep. TO HIM THE PORTER OPENETH; and the sheep hear his voice: and he calleth his own sheep by name, and leadeth them out.

John 10:2-3

10. *Become a good shepherd by providing spiritual insight for the sheep.* A shepherd must be one step ahead of the sheep in every area. You must have knowledge and wisdom to share with your sheep. A shepherd who has no time for reading and acquiring knowledge will never make a good pastor. Your authority over the people you lead is based on your ability to feed them with knowledge and understanding above what they have.

THIS PARABLE SPAKE JESUS UNTO THEM: but they understood not what things they were which he spake unto them.

John 10:6

11. *Become a good shepherd by making your sheep know your voice.* "The sheep follow him: for they know his voice" (John 10:4).

Some pastors do not preach much on Sundays because they share their pulpit democratically with others. They do this in the name of humility and fairness. For whatever reason, some pastors also rarely preach at their own weekday services. All these "humble" reasons for not preaching much cause the sheep not to hear the shepherd's voice regularly. Because of this, they do not get to know their own shepherd's voice. Your sheep will know your voice because they are used to your voice! They become used to your voice because they hear you often. This is why you must preach many, many messages to your sheep. The sheep need to get used to your voice. When they are used to your voice, your voice will be the most reassuring and comforting voice to them in the darkest hours of their lives. When the sheep know your voice, your voice will be the one they will obey in the most critical moments of their lives. Your voice will be the most believable voice amongst the many voices in their lives.

...AND THE SHEEP HEAR HIS VOICE: and he calleth his own sheep by name, and leadeth them out.
                                                      John 10:3

MY SHEEP HEAR MY VOICE,
                                                      John 10:27

12. *Become a good shepherd by calling your own sheep by name.* A good shepherd must know the names of the sheep. One of the tasks of a shepherd is to learn the names of every single member. You must strive earnestly to know the names of everyone. No one enjoys being a nameless figure or just another statistic. No one enjoys being hissed at or being referred to by his problem.

Many times, people's names are forgotten and their problems are used as names. For instance, the pastor may say "Bring me the woman with the issue of blood," or "Where is the lady whose child died last week?" or "How is the brother whose chickens were eaten by a cat?"

Also, no one enjoys being referred to by some vague and name like, "the upstairs people" or "the foreigners". Learn the names of people and they will love you just for that.

...HE CALLETH HIS OWN SHEEP BY NAME, and leadeth them out.

John 10:3

13. *Become a good shepherd by leading your own sheep to good pastures.* Every good shepherd must do whatever he can to ensure that his sheep have lots of food. Sometimes you cannot feed the sheep yourself but you must be able to organise good food for them. A good shepherd invites ministers to preach and bless his congregation. This is what the good shepherd does. He leads them to the green pasture.

...he calleth his own sheep by name, AND LEADETH THEM OUT.

John 10:3

14. *Become a good shepherd by going before your own sheep as you lead them out.* Being a good shepherd involves going out ahead of the sheep. Everybody is looking for a good example to follow. There are many teachers with great principles to offer. The reality is that there are much fewer good examples of people who have lived out these principles. Lead the way in life. Lead the way in marriage. Lead the way into prosperity. Go out before your own sheep and they will follow you.

And when he putteth forth his own sheep, HE GOETH BEFORE THEM, and the sheep follow him: for they know his voice.

John 10:4

15. *Become a good shepherd by making the sheep follow you.* Leadership involves making people follow you. You may be prayerful but unable to make the people in the church pray. You may be sacrificial but unable to make others sacrifice for the Lord. A good shepherd is able to make the sheep follow him wherever he goes.

One day, I spoke to a great man of God who had accomplished many things in ministry. He had become a missionary and had accomplished many things for the Lord. But he admitted, "I cannot get the people in my large church to become missionaries like I did."

I was saddened by the reality that a shepherd could not get his sheep to follow him.

And when he putteth forth his own sheep, he goeth before them, AND THE SHEEP FOLLOW HIM: for they know his voice.

John 10:4

My sheep hear my voice, and I know them, and they follow me:

John 10:27

16. *Become a good shepherd by having the sheep recognize your voice.* Recognition of the shepherd's voice is a vital aspect in the development of the sheep. When someone says, "I visit all churches. They are all the same. A church is a church. Every church worships God. It is all the same thing," he reveals that he has never been a true member of any church, or a sheep of any shepherd.

A true sheep will be able to recognize the voice of his shepherd and will have discovered that all churches and shepherds are not the same. A true sheep will know the differences between the different voices of shepherds.

And when he putteth forth his own sheep, he goeth before them, and the sheep follow him: FOR THEY KNOW HIS VOICE.

John 10:4

17. *Become a good shepherd by being the door of the sheep.* Being a door for the sheep speaks of providing an entrance for the sheep to move forward. A good shepherd provides a way for the sheep to enter many different things. A good shepherd provides a way for the sheep to enter into marriage. You make a way for your sheep to enter into marriage by teaching about marriage and counselling them.

A shepherd makes a way for his sheep to enter a prosperous life through his teaching and his guidance. A good shepherd makes a way for his sheep to enter the ministry. This is how a shepherd is a door to the sheep.

Then said Jesus unto them again, Verily, verily, I say unto you, I AM THE DOOR OF THE SHEEP.

John 10:7

I am the door:

John 10:9

18. *Become a good shepherd by providing salvation for the sheep.* A good shepherd goes out to find the lost sheep. Going out to find lost sheep is called evangelism. A good shepherd must be deeply involved in evangelism. Every good shepherd causes people to saved through his ministry. A good shepherd starts his work by bringing people to Christ and thereafter pastoring them. When you pastor people who were saved through your ministry, you will find that they are even more stable and faithful to you. Unfortunately, many pastors have lost the skills of evangelism and expect their churches to grow from their poaching activities in other congregations.

I am the door: by me IF ANY MAN ENTER IN, HE SHALL BE SAVED, and shall go in and out, and find pasture.

John 10:9

19. *Become a good shepherd by giving life to the sheep.* Through a good pastor, the sheep experience a better kind of life. The teachings that bring wisdom and understanding give the sheep a better life. Most sheep would not have a good life without the input of their shepherd and pastor.

...I AM COME THAT THEY MIGHT HAVE LIFE, and that they might have it more abundantly.

John 10:10

20. *Become a good shepherd by giving your life for the sheep.* In addition to giving the sheep a better life, the shepherd actually

lays down his life in order that the sheep have a better life. He uses his life as an example to help the sheep get along. He sacrifices many things in order that the sheep may have a better life. Many shepherds do not make sacrifices for their congregations but the rank of a shepherd, is carved out by the sacrifices he makes for his congregation.

...the good shepherd GIVETH HIS LIFE FOR THE SHEEP.

John 10:11

...I lay down my life for the sheep.

John 10:15

Therefore doth my Father love me, because I lay down my life, that I might take it again.

John 10:17

21. *Become a good shepherd by being the opposite of a hireling.* It takes almost nothing for a hireling to abandon his sheep. But a real shepherd will not easily leave the sheep. He gives his entire life to shepherding because he is not just a hired hand.

But he that is an hireling, and not the shepherd, whose own the sheep are not, seeth the wolf coming, and leaveth the sheep, and fleeth: and the wolf catcheth them, and scattereth the sheep. THE HIRELING FLEETH, because he is an hireling, and careth not for the sheep.

John 10:12-13

22. *Become a good shepherd by acting as the owner of the sheep.* Having an ownership mentality about anything transforms it. This is the reason for the worldwide privatization of many government-owned businesses. Anything that is not owned by specific people is not cared for or managed properly. God wants every shepherd to treat the sheep with the love and care of an owner and not with the mind of a heartless employee.

But he that is an hireling, and not the shepherd, WHOSE OWN THE SHEEP ARE not, seeth the wolf coming, and leaveth the sheep, and fleeth: and the wolf catcheth them, and scattereth the sheep.

John 10:12

23. *Become a good shepherd by noticing when the sheep are in danger.* Someone who does not love you will not even notice when you are in mortal danger. Most people just think about themselves. You would be surprised to know that people care more about their headache than about your cancer! A good shepherd notices when his sheep are in distress. Even little things are picked up by a good shepherd. Unfortunately a hireling does not even see when the sheep are dying.

But he that is an hireling, and not the shepherd, whose own the sheep are not, SEETH THE WOLF COMING, and leaveth the sheep, and fleeth: and the wolf catcheth them, and scattereth the sheep.

John 10:12

24. *Become a good shepherd by staying with the sheep in times of trouble.* A shepherd must be there when the trouble is at its peak. The shepherd must be found standing by the grave, in the hospital, at the operating theatre, by the bedside or wherever the trouble has struck. Bad shepherds visit the sheep to get money from them, when they are rich. But good shepherds are there in times of trouble.

But he that is an hireling, and not the shepherd, whose own the sheep are not, seeth the wolf coming, and LEAVETH THE SHEEP, and fleeth: and the wolf catcheth them, and scattereth the sheep.

John 10:12

25. *Become a good shepherd by knowing your sheep intimately.* In this discourse about the good shepherd, Jesus emphasizes how the shepherd knows the sheep. This knowledge becomes more intimate and more detailed as life goes on.

Pastors often realise that they never really knew their sheep, when they discover amazing truths about their sheep after years of pastoring them. You will discover that intimate detailed knowledge of each and every sheep is a must for real shepherding work.

I am the good shepherd, AND KNOW MY SHEEP, and am known of mine.

John 10:14

My sheep hear my voice, AND I KNOW THEM, and they follow me:

John 10:27

26. *Become a good shepherd by being known by your sheep.* The confidence of sheep is built up the more they know their shepherd. You cannot pastor a congregation by being a mystical figure. The sheep want to participate in your victories, defeats, sorrows and joys. All these help them to realize that you are genuine and that your words can be trusted.

I am the good shepherd, and know my sheep, and AM KNOWN OF MINE.

John 10:14

27. *Become a good shepherd by knowing the Father.* Becoming intimate with the heavenly Father is key to developing spiritual power. The presence of God rests on the person who abides in the secret place of the Most High. Shepherding is a spiritual job and closeness to the Father is essential.

As the Father knoweth me, EVEN SO KNOW I THE FATHER: and I lay down my life for the sheep.

John 10:15

28. *Become a good shepherd by being known by the Father.* Being open and frank with God is part of the spiritual development necessary to be a good shepherd. God knows everything, but you must come to Him and bare your soul

before Him. In so doing, you will draw close to the presence of God. Being close to the presence of God makes you a good shepherd.

As THE FATHER KNOWETH ME, even so know I the Father: and I lay down my life for the sheep.

John 10:15

29. *Become a good shepherd by having other sheep in other folds.* Part of the natural development of a shepherd's work is to develop sheep in other folds. Having congregations in different locations is an important development in your shepherding profile. Do not be afraid to establish branches. Your members will move away, anyway. You might as well develop congregations in different locations so that when they travel they will have somewhere to worship.

And OTHER SHEEP I HAVE, which are not of this fold: them also I must bring, and they shall hear my voice; and there shall be one fold, and one shepherd.

John 10:16

30. *Become a good shepherd by bringing in other sheep through evangelism.* Being a good shepherd means you must do the work of an evangelist. This is exactly what Paul admonished Timothy to do when he left him in charge of the flock. "But watch thou in all things, endure afflictions, do the work of an evangelist, make full proof of thy ministry" (2 Timothy 4:5).

And other sheep I have, which are not of this fold: THEM ALSO I MUST BRING, and they shall hear my voice; and there shall be one fold, and one shepherd.

John 10:16

31. *Become a good shepherd by pulling together your sheep from other folds.* This speaks of regularly gathering your congregations in different places into one large fold so that you can speak to them and so that they can hear your voice.

It is important that the different congregations which are linked to you are assembled frequently to listen to your voice. You must fight those who oppose these gatherings because it is the will of God to gather the sheep from other folds into one for the singular purpose of them hearing your words.

And other sheep I have, which are not of this fold: them ALSO I MUST BRING, AND THEY SHALL HEAR MY VOICE; and there shall be one fold, and one shepherd.

John 10:16

32. *Become a good shepherd by being the one shepherd in charge of the fold.* It is important for the sheep to recognize one leader. There cannot be two captains on one ship. Do not allow ambiguity to develop in your leadership. Let everyone be sure about who the leader is. Allowing the sheep to recognize one shepherd in one fold only serves to bind us together in unity and to fight confusion in the body.

And other sheep I have, which are not of this fold: them also I must bring, and they shall hear my voice; and there shall be ONE FOLD, AND ONE SHEPHERD.

John 10:16

33. *Become a good shepherd by taking up your life again after you have laid it down.* A good shepherd must not only know how to sacrifice but also how to take up the benefits due him as the shepherd of the sheep. This is exemplified by Christ who lay down His life, but also took it again. These two activities are completely opposite to each other, but there is a time and a season for each of them.

Therefore doth my Father love me, because I lay down my life, THAT I MIGHT TAKE IT AGAIN.

John 10:17

34. *Become a good shepherd by giving up your life freely and of your own initiative.* A good shepherd needs no one to tell him when and how to make the necessary sacrifices. Sacrifice is

necessary all the time, but sacrifice loses its power when you are forced to sacrifice by circumstances.

Sometimes, people decide to work for the Lord only after a serious illness strikes them. Before this illness, they were unwilling to make certain sacrifices, but when they sensed the inevitable, they seemed very willing to do anything for the Lord. But we all know that being forced to do something is different from doing it willingly. Serving the Lord at gunpoint, is obviously different from serving Him willingly. At gunpoint, you will run, jump and smile but we all know that your smiles are fake! Decide to lay down your life freely and willingly. Do it when you are young. Do it when you are strong. Do it when you are well! God is not a man. He is not deceived by things that are not real!

NO MAN TAKETH IT FROM ME, but I lay it down of myself. I have power to lay it down, and I have power to take it again. This commandment have I received of my Father.

John 10:18

35. *Become a good shepherd by recognizing the power you have to affect lives.* When you are a good shepherd, God will entrust you with much authority. This authority gives you the power to bring life or to bring death to many lives. Use that power wisely. God will judge you for everything He gives you.

No man taketh it from me, but I lay it down of myself. I HAVE POWER to lay it down, and I have power to take it again. This commandment have I received of my Father.

John 10:18

Chapter 28

How to Engage Your Sheep with Different Types of Relationships

To be a good shepherd you must engage the sheep and lock them into a relationship with you. Therefore, to be a truly good shepherd and leader, you must be able to develop *good, engaging relationships* with people. Unsuccessful pastors often lack the ability to develop deep engaging relationships.

The relationship-making ability of a person often defines his pastoral ministry. Some pastors simply do not have enough relationship-making abilities to build a family around them.

A pastor once described his friendship with me.

He said, "I have a *relationship* with Dag."

What he was trying to say was that he had a deep relationship with me. But I didn't think we had a deep relationship at all. In fact, I felt we had a very shallow relationship.

He was someone I would invite to minister at different church conferences, but I never thought of him as someone with whom I had a deep relationship.

As you can see, we had completely different assessments of our relationship. One person felt the relationship was deep and the other felt the relationship was almost non-existent. We understood relationships in completely different ways based on our backgrounds and perceptions. Indeed, the different kinds of relationships we maintained, played out in the kind of ministries that we had developed.

Basically, the depth of your relationships depends on what you know or understand about relationships. Some people know of only one kind of relationship. They do not know about other kinds of relationships that *engage the sheep* so they never develop those.

Some people can only relate as a master to a servant because that is all they have ever seen. Some people can only relate with ladies in a sexual way because that is all they have ever known as far as male-female relationships are concerned.

Some people cannot develop close relationships because they have never been open and free with others. Such people constantly maintain veils around different aspects of their lives. Our backgrounds and past experiences greatly fashion the kinds of relationships we are able to develop. Let me share with you twelve different kinds of relationships through which you can engage the sheep.

1. Engage Your Sheep through "Close-Friend" Relationships

And the LORD spake unto Moses face to face, as a man speaketh unto HIS FRIEND. And he turned again into the camp: but his servant Joshua, the son of Nun, a young man, departed not out of the tabernacle.

Exodus 33:11

Which forsaketh the guide of her youth, and forgetteth the covenant of her God.

Proverbs 2:17

The word "friend" comes from the Hebrew word *rea.* It means an associate who is close, a brother, a companion, a fellow or a neighbour. Pastors need close and deep friendships to engage the sheep.

To tend a flock is the Hebrew word *ra`ah* which means to associate with someone as a friend. Therefore becoming friends with people is a way of pastoring them. When you develop friendships with people, you are opening for yourself a door into their lives. For successful pastoral work, you need to have deep relationships that engage the lives of people. For successful pastoral work, you need to be involved in some intimate aspects of people's lives. After all, the shepherd is there to solve problems and if the problems cannot be talked about, or even mentioned, how is the shepherd going to work?

When you do not have deep relationships, you live in a world of delusions. You think everything is alright when it is not. You think you know people when you do not know them at all. You think there are no problems only because they are never talked about! When you do not have deep relationships, you lack the understanding necessary for real pastoral work. The lack of deep relationships will prevent you from developing a nuclear family that will grow into a large congregation.

One of the dangers of not developing deep relationships is the inability to recognize brewing disloyalty. Because your relationships are superficial, you will not notice when people do not like you or believe in you. Do not be deceived by the civilities and perfunctory politeness of the people. Courtesies and good manners are no substitute for loyalty.

I remember a pastor who was completely shocked by the sudden abandonment and betrayal of his associates. This fellow had a formal style of relating. He was more into protocol and other forms of proper behaviour. Because of this, he lacked the ability to develop a certain depth of relationship.

One of the deepest kinds of relationships is the relationship between friends. Pastors and leaders need to develop friendships that go beyond the formalities and civilities. Your friend cannot easily betray you! Your associate who has become your friend and who sticks closer than a brother is safer to have around than your associate who relates to you like a menial servant.

Ministers must develop deep friendships in order to engage their sheep. Relationships between senior pastors and their associates will be greatly enhanced if deep friendships are developed. Pastor-congregation relationships will be enhanced if real friendships are developed. Develop deep friendships with people who are important to your life and ministry.

2. Engage Your Sheep through "Master-Servant" Relationships

But which of you, having a servant plowing or feeding cattle, will say unto him by and by, when he is come

from the field, Go and sit down to meat? And will not rather say unto him, Make ready wherewith I may sup, and gird thyself, and serve me, till I have eaten and drunken; and afterward thou shalt eat and drink?

Luke 17:7-8

This kind of relationship is the type where the senior partner in the relationship relates like a lord with his servant. The advantage of this kind of relationship is that rank is not disregarded or despised. This type of relationship emphasizes "rank" and "differences." In the Scripture above, the servant has a completely different life from the master. Whilst the master rests, the servant works and sweats. The differences are made clear by everything that happens between the master and servant. When rank and differences are emphasized they help with the development of order. Unfortunately, this orderliness does not prevent incipient disloyalty.

The master-servant relationship can also generate a lot of fear. There is a lot of fear of losing your job or losing your favour. The fear of losing favour causes people to become hypocrites and pretenders. A pastor who has mostly master-servant relationships can easily be surrounded by hypocrites, pretenders and liars who do not love him at all.

You never know what your servant is thinking about you. You never know whether your servant wants to kill you or not. Your servant is more likely to kill you than your friend. King Amon and King Joash were killed by their servants and not by their friends.

The following Scriptures show how the servants of King Amon killed him.

Amon was twenty and two years old when he began to reign, and he reigned two years in Jerusalem. And his mother's name was Meshullemeth, the daughter of Haruz of Jotbah. And he did that which was evil in the sight of the LORD, as his father Manasseh did.
And he walked in all the way that his father walked in, and served the idols that his father served, and worshipped

them: And he forsook the LORD God of his fathers, and walked not in the way of the LORD.

AND THE SERVANTS OF AMON CONSPIRED AGAINST HIM, AND SLEW THE KING IN HIS OWN HOUSE.

And the people of the land slew all them that had conspired against king Amon; and the people of the land made Josiah his son king in his stead.

2 Kings 21:19-24

On another occasion, King Joash was also killed by his servants.

Thus Joash the king remembered not the kindness which Jehoiada his father had done to him, but slew his son. And when he died, he said, The LORD look upon it, and require it.

And it came to pass at the end of the year, that the host of Syria came up against him: and they came to Judah and Jerusalem, and destroyed all the princes of the people from among the people, and sent all the spoil of them unto the king of Damascus.

For the army of the Syrians came with a small company of men, and the LORD delivered a very great host into their hand, because they had forsaken the LORD God of their fathers. So they executed judgment against Joash.

And when they were departed from him, (for they left him in great diseases,) HIS OWN SERVANTS CONSPIRED AGAINST HIM FOR THE BLOOD OF THE SONS OF JEHOIADA THE PRIEST, AND SLEW HIM ON HIS BED, AND HE DIED: and they buried him in the city of David, but they buried him not in the sepulchres of the kings.

And these are they that conspired against him; Zabad the son of Shimeath an Ammonitess, and Jehozabad the son of Shimrith a Moabitess.

2 Chronicles 24:22-26

How would you know who is conspiring against you if you sit up in your castle and look down below to your servants? How will you know what your servants are thinking if they are not your friends? Do you want to become another of many kings whose servants conspired against them and killed them?

3. Engage Your Sheep through "Bride-Groom" Relationships

Husbands, love your wives, even as Christ also loved the church, and gave himself for it; That he might sanctify and cleanse it with the washing of water by the word,

Ephesians 5:25-26

Bride-groom relationships are passionate relationships which engage the sheep. Passion is usually based on mystery about who the other party is. Brides and grooms are passionately in love with each other largely because they are unfamiliar with each other. The mystery of each other creates much excitement and draws them together.

Obviously, every pastoral relationship needs a bit of this passionate feel. The absence of passion leads to the absence of zeal. A relationship which lacks passion is dull and routine and cannot engage the sheep. You must be excited about your ministry to the sheep. You must have energy and zeal to follow up on sheep even if they do not appreciate you. Young people have this passion and zeal for ministry and they often have better bride-groom relationships.

4. Engage Your Sheep through "Father-Son" Relationships

My son, hear the instruction of thy father, and forsake not the law of thy mother:

Proverbs 1:8

Another way a pastor can engage his sheep is by developing a father-son relationship. This is a deeper kind of relationship in which the pastor begins to treat the sheep as his own children. A family develops and the pastor provides and cares for his sheep as a father would for his sons and daughters. There is counsel, there is guidance and there is direction for the sheep in a loving assuring way. This kind of relationship is far stronger than an employer-employee relationship. It is deeper and achieves more because of the greater trust and obedience

Hear, O my son, and receive my sayings; and the years of thy life shall be many.

Proverbs 4:10

My son, attend to my words; incline thine ear unto my sayings.

Proverbs 4:20

My son, keep thy father's commandment, and forsake not the law of thy mother:

Proverbs 6:20

5. Engage Your Sheep through "Teacher-Disciple" Relationships

Verily, verily, I say unto you, the servant is not greater than his lord; neither he that is sent greater than he that sent him.

John 13:16

This is the type of relationship in which there is a lot of training. Great authority is established over the people because of constant teaching and training. You will develop unbelievable authority if you are able to teach your sheep.

The more areas you are able to teach on, the more your authority deepens. There are different reasons why people may not teach on certain areas. Sometimes, pastors are simply ignorant in certain fields and cannot make any comments on certain issues. Sometimes pastors have no idea about political, financial or leadership issues. They seem to only understand the Bible.

Sometimes pastors are too shy to teach on certain issues in marriage. Because they do not teach on certain subjects, their authority is limited. Some pastors are also unable to develop a relationship with their associates in which they teach them the word of God. They are unable to look people in the eye and teach them in a small group setting. This also limits their ability to control and lead their associates. It is important for you to develop a teacher-disciple relationship with everyone you are leading.

6. Engage Your Sheep through "Husband-Wife" Relationships

Husbands, love your wives, even as Christ also loved the church, and gave himself for it;
Ephesians 5:25

You can also engage your sheep with what I call a husband-wife relationship. This kind of relationship is a permanent family relationship. It involves relating with people as a permanent family with whom you will live until you die. It is starkly contrasted with the kind of relationship where you are employed for a couple of years until you get a better offer.

The husband-wife relationship is a very domestic one. When you develop this kind of relationship, you have domestic dealings with people. This brings your members closer and makes their lives intertwined with yours. But beware, these kind of relationships can become too close!

7. Engage Your Sheep through "Head-Body" Relationships

And he is before all things, and by him all things consist. And he is the head of the body, the church: who

is the beginning, the firstborn from the dead; that in all things he might have the preeminence.

Colossians 1:17-18

In head-body relationships the body trusts the head to take decisions and lead the way. In this kind of relationship, the shepherd has to take decisions that will change the lives and future of the sheep.

Some pastors do not have this kind of relationship but create a democratic culture in their churches. Democracy is good, but it can kill the leading of the Spirit. It also kills the head-body relationship that is necessary for rapid growth.

Indeed, it is a necessary type of relationship if the whole congregation is to move forward in the will of God.

8. Engage Your Sheep through "Vine-Branch" Relationships

I am the vine, ye are the branches: He that abideth in me, and I in him, the same bringeth forth much fruit: for without me ye can do nothing.

John 15:5

The vine-branch relationship speaks of the deepest level of inter-connection, which leads to the highest type of fruit-bearing. When the branches are completely merged with the vine, they bring forth fruit. There is a way in which you can completely merge with your leader until your voice merges with his voice and your ways with his ways. When this happens, you are ready to bear the highest kind of fruit.

Deep interactive relationships result in the transfer of anointings and other important impartations. Have a vision to develop close relationships until lives and visions virtually merge into each other.

9. Engage Your Sheep through "Husbandman-Vineyard" Relationships

What could have been done more to my vineyard, that I have not done in it? wherefore, when I looked that it should bring forth grapes, brought it forth wild grapes?

And now go to; I will tell you what I will do to my vineyard: I will take away the hedge thereof, and it shall be eaten up; and break down the wall thereof, and it shall be trodden down:

And I will lay it waste: it shall not be pruned, nor digged; but there shall come up briers and thorns: I will also command the clouds that they rain no rain upon it.

Isaiah 5:4-6

The husbandman-vineyard relationship involves nurturing someone until he is fruitful. It also involves developing the ability to prune and cut away unwanted elements, which hinder fruitfulness. This type of relationship involves the unpleasant cutting away of unwanted people.

A good shepherd must develop strong fellowships. To develop strong fellowships you will have to remove accusers, complainers, backbiters, slanderers and discontented people. If you cannot develop this aspect of "pastoral engagement", you will endanger the rest of your followers. Your failure to remove the one bad apple will cause all the other apples to become rotten. Disloyalty is a spiritual emergency that needs to be dealt with quickly.

10. Engage Your Sheep through "Potter-Clay" Relationships

Surely your turning of things upside down shall be esteemed as the potter's clay: for shall the work say of him that made it, He made me not? Or shall the thing framed say of him that framed it, He had no understanding?

Isaiah 29:16

In this kind of relationship, the pastor is constantly moulding people into vessels, which can be used by the Lord. Moulding a vessel goes one step further than teaching does. The teacher-disciple relationship involves only teaching. But this kind of relationship involves the total transformation of a person by the shepherd. The whole life of the sheep is changed through "potter-clay engagement".

It is not about having had a lesson; it is about an entire life being remoulded into something special. I am sure you can see that this involves more than receiving a few teachings and writing a few notes. You may be made to do certain things that change your life until you are unrecognizable by people who knew you in the past. Do not be afraid to develop this kind of relationship.

One night during a church service, I began to pray for people and lay hands on them. When I laid hands on a particular person, I began to weep uncontrollably. Later, I wondered what had made me cry so much when I laid hands on that person. Then it came to me; this person's life would be changed forever. This individual was not just going to receive a few nice teachings but a major change in his life. Everything was about to change in his life because he was about to go on the mission field. Everything changes when the potter works on the clay. If you have a potter-clay relationship, expect absolute transformation.

11. Engage Your Sheep through "Commander-Troops" Relationships

And he said, Nay; but as captain of the host of the LORD am I now come. And Joshua fell on his face to the earth, and did worship, and said unto him, What saith my lord unto his servant? And the captain of the LORD'S host said unto Joshua, Loose thy shoe from off thy foot; for the place whereon thou standest is holy. And Joshua did so.

Joshua 5:14-15

You can engage your people as a commander engages his troops. There is a military style of leadership that is needed to make your pastoral ministry comprehensive. After your church has grown, it is important to be able to command your members to go into the world and make disciples.

To develop a commander's relationship you will need to teach your people about sacrifice. The army is a highly disciplined force in which people are ready to die as easily as a civilian drinks water. When a congregation is trained to make sacrifices, it will.

After all, Christianity is based on the concept of sacrifice. The words, "Take up your cross and follow Jesus" must become popular in your congregation.

When the commander-troops relationship is developed you will say to one, "Go" and he goeth; and to another, "Come" and he cometh. You will ask the people to go anywhere or do anything and they will do it because you said so.

12. Engage Your Sheep through "Creator-Creature" Relationships

...for shall the work say of him that made it, He made me not? or shall the thing framed say of him that framed it, He had no understanding?

Isaiah 29:16

This kind of pastoral relationship is similar to the potter-clay relationship. It is all about making something out of nothing. A pastor must specialise in making great people out of nobodies. That is what God did when He created this beautiful world from a formless void. Pastors must be able to see gems within ordinary people. Often when a pastor does not have certain gifted people in his church, it is because he never saw the gems within the ordinary people. You will have to learn the art of turning raw materials into valuable finished products.

Chapter 29

Twelve Characteristics of Hireling Shepherds

Hirelings are people who work for money. Their desire for money dominates everything they do. They may have no need for money, but cannot relate with you unless it has to do with a financial exchange of some sort.

Hirelings cannot imagine anyone doing something for free. Jesus specifically mentioned hirelings as not being good for the sheep. It is important to fully understand how hirelings operate so that we will not become hirelings.

1. Hirelings always ask for money.

They that were FULL have hired out themselves for bread...

$\qquad$ **1 Samuel 2:5**

Hirelings love money so much that even when they do not need it they still ask for it. They cannot imagine doing the simplest job without charging heavily for it. The Scripture below shows us that hirelings were full. In other words, they did not need to eat anything. And yet they wanted to be paid with bread. Is it not amazing that sometimes the richest people are the greatest thieves? They have enough and yet they want more.

2. Hirelings build churches for money.

...and HIRED masons and carpenters to repair the house of the LORD...

$\qquad$ **2 Chronicles 24:12**

They build the church and do the work of preaching, teaching, visiting and interacting, expecting money for their work. You must desire to build God's house out of gratitude for your salvation. You must build God's house out of your love for Him and not out of your desire for money.

3. Hirelings help around the church for money.

> ...and hired...also such as wrought iron and brass to mend the house of the LORD..
>
> 2 Chronicles 24:12

Once again, hirelings love to help around but they want a full payment for every hour they worked. Such people receive payment for doing odd jobs in church like playing instruments, decorating the church and helping around.

4. Hirelings can easily become disloyal.

> **And the princes of the children of Ammon said unto Hanun their lord, Thinkest thou that David doth honour thy father, that he hath sent comforters unto thee? hath not David rather sent his servants unto thee, to search the city, and to spy it out, and to overthrow it?**
>
> **Wherefore Hanun took David's servants, and shaved off the one half of their beards, and cut off their garments in the middle, even to their buttocks, and sent them away.**
>
> **When they told it unto David, he sent to meet them, because the men were greatly ashamed: and the king said, Tarry at Jericho until your beards be grown, and then return.**
>
> **And when the children of Ammon saw that they stank before David, the children of Ammon sent and hired the Syrians of Beth-rehob, and the Syrians of Zoba, twenty thousand footmen, and of king Maacah a thousand**
>
> **And when David heard of it, he sent Joab, and all the host of the mighty men.**
>
> **And the children of Ammon came out, and put the battle in array at the entering in of the gate: and the Syrians of Zoba, and of Rehob, and Ish-tob, and Maacah, were by themselves in the field.**
>
> **When Joab saw that the front of the battle was against him before and behind, he chose of all the choice men**

of Israel, and put them in array against the Syrians:

And the rest of the people he delivered into the hand of Abishai his brother, that he might put them in array against the children of Ammon.

And he said, If the Syrians be too strong for me, then thou shalt help me: but if the children of Ammon be too strong for thee, then I will come and help thee.

2 Samuel 10:3-11

Hirelings want money so they can be hired for almost any frivolous cause. This means they can also desert you for many foolish reasons. They can fight for any cause or any side, depending on who pays more. If you hire someone with a hireling spirit, you never know when he is undergoing negotiations with your enemies.

You can see in the Scripture below how the children of Ammon were able to hire the Syrians to come and fight a senseless war for them. They went to war over an issue involving the beards of David's servants being shaved off. Such is the nature of the hireling. Once there is money to be earned they will do anything.

5. Hirelings always think that others are thinking about money.

For the Lord had made the host of the Syrians to hear a noise of chariots, and a noise of horses, even the noise of a great host: and they said one to another, Lo, the king of Israel hath HIRED against us the kings of the Hittites, and the kings of the Egyptians, to come upon us.

2 Kings 7:6

Being hirelings, they think that every minister preaches for money. They expect that every other minister will love money the way they do. In the Scripture below, the Syrians expected that the king of Israel would hire people to fight against him. He needed no one to tell him that there were soldiers who were ready to fight for whatever reason, once they were paid for it.

6. Hirelings are useless to God.

...wherewith Abimelech hired VAIN and light persons, which followed him.

Judges 9:4

The Bible describes hirelings as "vain", which means "useless." A minister whose main motivation is money is not valuable to God. A hireling is basically under the influence of money. God does not lead hirelings; money does! Hirelings do not take instructions from God. They receive orders from money. This is why a hireling is useless to God. A hireling is useful to the god of money but is not useful to the living God.

7. Hirelings are shallow.

...wherewith Abimelech hired vain and LIGHT PERSONS, which followed him.

Judges 9:4

Hirelings are people who are not deep, spiritually. The Bible describes them as "light". A deep person will not charge God for services rendered. If you think deeply about it, you will realise that there is nothing we can claim that belongs to us. At best, we are privileged to use something for a period. Everything we have is a gift from God. To make God chargeable for what you have is a deception of the highest order. If you fear God, you will tremble at the thought of extorting any kind of money from a church.

8. Money is the god of hirelings.

...and hire a goldsmith; and HE MAKETH IT A GOD: they fall down, yea, they worship.

Isaiah 46:6

Money becomes the god of a hireling. Money can make a hireling do anything. You serve either God or mammon! It is interesting that the Scripture declares that the alternative to God is money. I would have thought that the devil would be the opposing alternative to God. But Jesus said we have to choose between God and money!

The whole world is manipulated by money! Satan is the god of this world and most of the wealth in the world is in the hands of evil men who are controlled by Satan.

This is why a person becomes detached from God when he works for money. Such is the lot of a hireling. He is detached from God and has made money his god.

9. Hirelings can be hired by rich men.

And he said unto them, Thus and thus dealeth Micah with me, and hath hired me, and I am his priest.

Judges 18:4

Hireling pastors often become personal prophets to rich people. Hireling pastors sing the praises of their rich bosses and prophesy only good news to them. To be a good pastor, you need to be independent of rich people who give you money.

10. Hirelings can easily disobey God.

Because they met not the children of Israel with bread and with water, but hired Balaam against them, that he should curse them: howbeit our God turned the curse into a blessing.

Nehemiah 13:2

Hirelings easily go against the will of God because of money. A hireling can even fight God Himself because of money. Balaam tried to curse people that God had blessed.

11. Hirelings are not directed by God but by money.

And, lo, I perceived that GOD HAD NOT SENT HIM; but that he pronounced this prophecy against me: for Tobiah and Sanballat had hired him. Therefore was he hired, that I should be afraid, and do so, and sin,

**and that they might have matter for an evil report, that
they might reproach me.**

Nehemiah 6:12-13

Hirelings have not been sent by God and are not called by
God. They are "called" by money. They have been "sent" by
money. The direction of a hireling's ministry is determined by
the amount of money to be earned.

They will not go even if there are souls to be won. If there
is money but no real ministry a hireling will go. All a hireling
wants is money.

I have watched as people have started churches for financial
reasons. They wanted to have a share of the offerings. They
wanted money and not God's will. Hirelings love to present
super-spiritual reasons for what they do. Sanballat and Tobiah
actually hired someone to prophesy. These people often speak of
how God has spoken to them. They say the Spirit is leading them
but often it is money that is leading them to destroy the church
that they helped to build.

12. Hirelings frustrate the work of God.

**And HIRED COUNSELLERS against them, TO
FRUSTRATE THEIR PURPOSE, all the days of Cyrus
king of Persia, even until the reign of Darius king of
Persia.**

Ezra 4:5

Because hirelings are not genuinely "called" and not a part
of genuine ministry, they actually frustrate true ministry. Even
the "world" is able to sense the greed in us when we preach for
money.

A good example of someone who frustrated true ministry was
Gehazi. Gehazi ministered for money and gave Commander
Naaman the impression that Elisha was greedy. In so doing, he
frustrated the work of God. There are pastors who worsen the
general impression that pastors are "just looking for money".
Surprisingly, the unbeliever commander, Naaman, saw through

the greed and covetousness of Gehazi and advised him to be content. "And he said, All is well. My master hath sent me, saying, Behold, even now there be come to me from mount Ephraim two young men of the sons of the prophets: give them, I pray thee, a talent of silver, and two changes of garments. And Naaman said, Be content, take two talents. And he urged him, and bound two talents of silver in two bags, with two changes of garments, and laid them upon two of his servants; and they bare them before him" (2 Kings 5:22-23).

Chapter 30

Nine Types of Hireling Pastors

A hireling is someone who *wants to receive money* when he works for God. All Christians are called to bear fruit and to work for God. Because of this, all categories of Christians and ministers can become hirelings.

Our lives, our money, our health and our very existence are what they are because God has allowed it. We owe everything to Him and therefore we cannot and should not charge Him for any services we render in His house. It is our greatest privilege to work for Him in any way. Every kind of service we are called upon to offer (technical, spiritual, financial, legal, musical), is an honour extended to us.

If we are looking for rewards, we should seek them in Heaven and not on earth! Heaven is the place for judgement, for rest and rewards! Earth is the place for work, work, work! If you insist on taking your rewards here, you may be forfeiting your heavenly reward.

Through my experiences in the church, I have encountered several different kinds of hirelings.

There are always people who wish to make a charge to the house of God. It is interesting how the Bible documents some of these different kinds of hirelings.

1. Rich hirelings

THEY THAT WERE FULL HAVE HIRED OUT THEMSELVES for bread; and they that were hungry ceased: so that the barren hath born seven; and she that hath many children is waxed feeble.

1 Samuel 2:5

These are people who do not need money but still charge for everything they do. The Scripture says they are full but they still hire themselves out for bread that they do not need. For instance, there may a rich architect or an engineer who does not need the church's money. However, he will insist on charging a professional fee for his work.

On the other hand, there may be a rich lawyer who does not need any money from the church but will insist on collecting his legal fees for drawing up a simple contract. Indeed these people are rich but still want to have bread given to them because they do not understand the concept of offering their services as a ministry to the Lord. There are also those who do not need to take a salary from the church but insist on taking their portion because they do not believe in doing anything free of charge.

2. *Technical Hirelings*

And the king and Jehoiada gave it to such as did the work of the service of the house of the LORD, and HIRED MASONS AND CARPENTERS to repair the house of the LORD, and also such as wrought iron and brass to mend the house of the LORD.

2 Chronicles 24:12

Technical hirelings refer to people who have some specialised skill and technical knowledge. Examples of these are pianists who charge the church for playing the piano on a Sunday. I have met people who charge for tuning the volume on the sound-mixer. There are also choristers who have to be paid to come for choir rehearsals.

There are plumbers and electricians who will not tighten a bolt in the church's toilet without charging a professional fee. Lawyers, doctors, engineers, architects all fall into this category of people with technical skill and knowledge. As the bible says, "what hast thou that thou didst not receive?" Everything we have and everything we know is a gift from God. If there is any way we can say thank you to the Lord by rendering some service to the ministry, let's do it with all our hearts.

3. Mercenary hirelings

And it came to pass after this, that the king of the children of Ammon died, and Hanun his son reigned in his stead. Then said David, I will shew kindness unto Hanun the son of Nahash, as his father shewed kindness unto me. And David sent to comfort him by the hand of his servants for his father. And David's servants came into the land of the children of Ammon. And the princes of the children of Ammon said unto Hanun their lord, Thinkest thou that David doth honour thy father, that he hath sent comforters unto thee? hath not David rather sent his servants unto thee, to search the city, and to spy it out, and to overthrow it? Wherefore Hanun took David's servants, and shaved off the one half of their beards, and cut off their garments in the middle, even to their buttocks, and sent them away. When they told it unto David, he sent to meet them, because the men were greatly ashamed: and the king said, Tarry at Jericho until your beards be grown, and then return. And when the children of Ammon saw that they stank before David, the children of Ammon sent and HIRED THE SYRIANS of Beth-rehob, and the Syrians of Zoba, twenty thousand footmen, and of king Maacah a thousand men, and of Ish-tob twelve thousand men.

2 Samuel 10:1-6

A mercenary is someone who is a professional soldier. He does not fight for honour or for a great national cause. He is someone who simply fights for money. An example of church mercenaries are prayer warriors and people who do battle in the spirit. Such people may pray only if you pay them a lot of money. There are also people who do evangelism just for the salary they will get. Prophets, pastors, teachers, are all examples of people who may fight the good fight of faith only for money.

For the Lord had made the host of the Syrians to hear a noise of chariots, and a noise of horses, even the noise of a great host: and they said one to another, Lo, the

king of Israel hath HIRED AGAINST US THE KINGS OF THE HITTITES, AND THE KINGS OF THE EGYPTIANS, TO COME UPON US.

2 Kings 7:6

4. Vain and light hirelings

And they gave him threescore and ten pieces of silver out of the house of Baal-berith, wherewith Abimelech HIRED VAIN AND LIGHT PERSONS, which followed him.

Judges 9:4

Vain and light hirelings are a large group of unspiritual people. They seldom see the eternal aspects of anything. Each time you are dealing with a church member, who is light or vain, his mind will work along certain lines.

Such people only see the church as a potential client to do business with. They will extract every dollar they can from the church. The spirit of lightness and vanity inspires this kind of hireling to get as much as he can from the church.

5. Counsellor hirelings

And hired counsellers against them, to frustrate their purpose, all the days of Cyrus king of Persia, even until the reign of Darius king of Persia.

Ezra 4:5

Once again, these are people who offer their counselling services to the Lord. They may be marriage counsellors or even teachers of the Word. Everything they do and everything they say has a bill attached to it.

It is important that we identify hirelings of every sort because Jesus did not speak well of hirelings. Jesus taught us that hirelings did not really care about the people they were looking after. Would you like to be looked after by a doctor who did not really care? The very nature of ministry changes when the ministers do not care.

6. False prophet hirelings

And, lo, I perceived that God had not sent him; but that he pronounced this prophecy against me: for Tobiah and Sanballat had hired him.

Nehemiah 6:12

One day, I visited a church that was pastored by a prophet. I realised the impact that the prophetic ministry had on the common people. Many of the church members were completely enchanted by this prophet who had amazingly accurate words of knowledge.

His amazing gift had drawn people who were far richer and far more educated than he was. I was impressed with the calibre of people who had been drawn to this illiterate prophet's ministry. I realised that his prophetic gift had overridden all his personal limitations.

I met one gentleman who told me how his life was literally transformed because the prophet had accurately informed him about how and when he was going to have a child.

It is easy to see how a true prophet like this can metamorphose into a false prophet. The more accurate the revelation that comes from the prophet, the more the prophet seems to benefit and the richer he seems to become.

There is therefore a temptation to come up with more fantastic prophecies and predictions since these may lead to a greater financial harvest for the prophet. This is how many true prophets have been transformed into false prophets. A false prophet is someone whose primary motivation is to get money. If money is your primary motivation, then you speak on behalf of money and not on behalf of God.

7. Famous hirelings

Because they met you not with bread and with water in the way, when ye came forth out of Egypt; and because THEY HIRED AGAINST THEE BALAAM the son of

Beor of Pethor of Mesopotamia, TO CURSE THEE.
Deuteronomy 23:4

Because they met not the children of Israel with bread and with water, but HIRED BALAAM AGAINST THEM, THAT HE SHOULD CURSE THEM: howbeit our God turned the curse into a blessing.
Nehemiah 13:2

Some hirelings gained their notoriety after having some really big contracts. Balaam the prophet was one such famous hireling. He is famous for having been hired to curse Israel when they were coming out of Egypt.

He is also famous for the fact that he was stopped in dramatic fashion by a donkey. Again, he is famous because his example proves that no one can curse what God has blessed. The example of Balaam also proves that a prophet who can be hired out for a few dollars is truly a false prophet.

8. *Pastoral hirelings*

And he said unto them, Thus and thus dealeth Micah with me, and hath HIRED ME, AND I AM HIS PRIEST.
Judges 18:4

There are also pastors whose services are available only for a fee. Such pastors will give specialized pastoral care to the richest person. You will notice how pastoral hirelings love to conduct private prayer meetings and Bible studies for rich members.

The ministry of Jesus is largely to the poor and must be available to those who cannot afford such specialized services. I wonder whether these hired pastors would tell their rich members the whole truth! It is not easy to rebuke an evil man when his very hand feeds you and your family.

9. *Associate Pastor Hirelings*

And he said, All is well. My master hath sent me, saying, Behold, even now there be come to me from

mount Ephraim two young men of the sons of the prophets: give them, I PRAY THEE, A TALENT OF SILVER, AND TWO CHANGES OF GARMENTS. And Naaman said, Be content, take two talents. And he urged him, and bound two talents of silver in two bags, with two changes of garments, and laid them upon two of his servants; and they bare them before him.

2 Kings 5:22-23

Gehazi is the classic assistant pastor who craves more money. He was the associate to Elisha and would have inherited the anointing that was on Elisha. His desire to earn money for ministering destroyed his future ministry.

Associate pastors can also be hired out for a fee. I remember one assistant pastor who was offered a higher salary. This pastor accepted the offer simply because it had a better financial package. Later on, he discovered that he had been employed by a crook. Are pastors simply looking for bigger salaries or are they trying to please God?

Chapter 31

Disappointing Shepherds

There are disappointments in the ministry. Many ministers of the Gospel start out with great expectation. They are appointed with great joy and expectation. But as time goes by, they become the greatest disappointments of the ministry. King Saul was the quintessential "disappointing shepherd". He was a great disappointment to the Prophet Samuel and also to the Lord. God regretted ever choosing him. Will you be a disappointment to the Lord one day?

Thirteen Signs of Disappointing Shepherds

I REGRET THAT I HAVE MADE SAUL KING, FOR HE HAS TURNED BACK FROM FOLLOWING ME AND HAS NOT CARRIED OUT MY COMMANDS. And Samuel was distressed and cried out to the LORD all night. Samuel rose early in the morning to meet Saul; and it was told Samuel, saying, "Saul came to Carmel, and behold, he set up a monument for himself, then turned and proceeded on down to Gilgal." Samuel came to Saul, and Saul said to him, "Blessed are you of the LORD! I have carried out the command of the LORD." But Samuel said, "What then is this bleating of the sheep in my ears, and the lowing of the oxen which I hear?"

1 Samuel 15:11-14 (NASB)

1. Disappointing pastors will make you regret that you appointed them.

    I REGRET THAT I HAVE MADE SAUL KING, for he has turned back from following Me and has not carried out My commands...

    1 Samuel 15:11(NASB)

The classic sign of a disappointing shepherd is that you will regret appointing him to the ministry. You will regret making him a pastor! You will regret ever introducing him to others as a minister of the Gospel! You will regret ordaining him to the ministry. I can clearly remember some people whom I wish I had never appointed as pastors. You must realise though that people do not intend to become disappointments and neither do they become disappointments overnight. As we shall see, there are reasons why people become disappointments in the ministry.

2. Disappointing shepherds follow their leader only to a point: they do not follow him completely.

I regret that I have made Saul king, for HE HAS TURNED BACK FROM FOLLOWING ME and has not carried out My commands...

1 Samuel 15:11

They follow half of the instructions and leave the other half. Following half-way will not lead you to the desired destination. Because people have failed to follow the Lord in totality, it looks as though it was a mistake to follow Him. Often, when people are appointed or ordained, they are deluded into thinking they have arrived. But no one has arrived! No one knows enough!

Until we get to heaven, we cannot say that anyone has borne enough fruit. We will be learners until we get to heaven. You must never think that you have arrived anywhere. Recently, the Lord told me that it was very dangerous to have the feeling that we needed nothing. "I have need of nothing" was the thought in the heart of the Laodecian church. "Get up and do something. Get up and buy something," he said to me. Don't tell yourself that you need nothing.

3. Disappointing shepherds do not follow the instructions and commands of their pastors.

I regret that I have made Saul king, for he has turned back from following Me and HAS NOT CARRIED OUT MY COMMANDS...

1 Samuel 15:11, NASB

I have watched as people have followed their own ideas and ended up nowhere. I remember assessing a group of missionaries that I had sent out. I had given them some instructions, which you could even call suggestions. Two of these missionaries followed the instructions completely and had large, successful growing churches.

The other missionaries struggled with a few people and with great financial difficulty. What was the difference between these missionaries? Two of them felt that my advice to them should be followed to the letter. The others did not try much to obey those instructions. Sometimes instructions given do not sound very spiritual but they are the very ones that may yield the largest dividends. Be careful to follow even the smallest detail of instructions and advice given by fathers who are more experienced than you.

Saul continued to argue with Samuel claiming to be doing the right thing in spite of the fact that he was obviously wrong. Saul said, "They have brought them from the Amalekites, for the people spared the best of the sheep and oxen, to sacrifice to the LORD your God; but the rest we have utterly destroyed" (1 Samuel 15:15).

Disappointing (Sauline) pastors never accept that they are wrong. They are self-deceived and will never admit wrongdoing. Even when there is evidence to the contrary, Sauline pastors do not repent. It is important to be able to say "sorry" when you are wrong. You are not called to the ministry because you are perfect. You are not called to the ministry because you will never make a mistake.

We abound in mistakes but God still uses us! There is no need to fight to maintain a perfect image. You are not perfect and neither am I. Saul continued to defend himself and reject the diagnoses of Samuel. This is what led to his destruction.

4. Disappointing shepherds choose the sacrifices they make.

Instead of obeying their pastor, they choose to do other sacrificial things. They therefore make sacrifices that are not acceptable, not required or not even wanted. Most employers have specific things that they expect from an employee. Usually, there are one or two very important things, which are required. It is always a mistake not to concentrate on those important instructions that will make the boss genuinely happy with you.

5. Disappointing pastors do not consider themselves as sheep once they have been appointed or ordained to the ministry.

Pastors still need to be led and still need to be guided. You must always consider yourself a little lamb. Disappointing pastors do not consider themselves as sheep anymore. It is important that you see yourself as a little sheep, constantly in need of direction. You need to be led and you need direction even if you are an ordained minister. I am constantly aware of my need for direction. Even though I have several churches under me, I am constantly praying for direction because it is the thing that I need most.

6. Disappointing shepherds do not remain small in their eyes.

Then Samuel said to Saul, "Wait, and let me tell you what the LORD said to me last night." And he said to him, "Speak!" Samuel said, "Is it not true, though you were little in your own eyes, you were made the head of the tribes of Israel? And the LORD anointed you king over Israel,"

1 Samuel 15:16-17 (NASB)

I always remember the words of a great man of God. He said, "My mother told me, 'stay small in your own eyes and you will be fine'." His mother had given him some of the best advice you could ever give to a pastor. Remain small, remain teachable, be a learner and be a nobody! In other words, do not be big. Do not be haughty. Do not be a know-it-all!

7. Disappointing shepherds argue and defend themselves, never understanding the point that is being made.

And the LORD sent you on a mission, and said, "Go and utterly destroy the sinners, the Amalekites, and fight against them until they are exterminated."

Why then did you not obey the voice of the LORD, but rushed upon the spoil and did what was evil in the sight of the LORD? Then Saul said to Samuel, "I DID OBEY THE VOICE OF THE LORD, and went on the mission on which the LORD sent me, and have brought back Agag the king of Amalek, and have utterly destroyed the Amalekites."

1 Samuel 15:18-20 (NASB)

To not understand, not agree, not see the point, not yield, not believe, not give up, not give in, is a symptom of a terrible spiritual disease. Saul had departed from the Lord in his heart and his disobedience was only a symptom. Saul was actually in rebellion. That spiritual condition is called disobedience, rebellion and witchcraft! Watch out for people who do not understand anything and never agree with the leader's point of view. Watch out for people who never admit their mistakes in spite of the evidence against them. Watch out for people you have to spend hours explaining the same thing to. Watch out for those who never change. Dangerous disappointing people never understand anything, never concede, never agree, never yield, never bend, never accept, never flow and never change!

8. **A disappointing shepherd blames the people for the problems in the church.**

"But the people took some of the spoil, sheep and oxen, the choicest of the things devoted to destruction, to sacrifice to the LORD your God at Gilgal."

1 Samuel 15:21 (NASB)

A good shepherd will blame *himself* for the failure of the congregation to grow. A "Sauline" shepherd will come up with all kinds of reasons why things are not working. A "Sauline" missionary will find a lot of problems with the country that he is sent to. He will see the natives of the country as problematic.

He will despise the country and the people that he is sent to, describing them as immoral, wicked and backward.

What he does not know is that all the peoples of the world are immoral, wicked and backward. That is why Christ sent us to them. It is because they need help that God sent us out as missionaries.

9. Disappointing shepherds are rebellious at heart.

They may not be openly rebellious but that is what they actually are. The disobedience, the inability to follow completely, the blaming of the people, the not remaining small in their own eyes, are all symptoms of rebellion.

For rebellion is as the sin of witchcraft, and stubbornness is as iniquity and idolatry...

1 Samuel 15:23

10. Disappointing pastors are like witches in the ministry.

For rebellion is as the sin of witchcraft, and stubbornness is as iniquity and idolatry...

1 Samuel 15:23

Witchcraft is the use of the use of a power other than the power of the Holy Spirit. Witchcraft deploys alternative powers to accomplish goals. Sauline shepherds are like witches who create a following within the larger group. They cause the ministry to go in a direction different from the leader's. Through stubbornness and disobedience, they have their way in the ministry, creating their own following within the larger group.

11. Disappointing shepherds fear the people rather than God.

Then Saul said to Samuel, "I have sinned; I have indeed transgressed the command of the LORD and your words, because I feared the people and listened to their voice."

1 Samuel 15:24 (NASB)

A sauline shepherd is like a politician. He is very concerned about what people think. In the ministry, you must be more concerned about what God thinks. The one thing that differentiates true ministry from false ministry is this singular ability to fear God rather than people.

If you are a man-fearing shepherd, your sermons will be affected and your decisions will be swayed because of the people. The less you fear people the higher you go in ministry. Jesus Christ's example of fearlessness is seen in His statement, "I receive not honour from men" (John 5:41).

In ministry, you must not fear your associate pastors. You must not fear your branch pastors. You must not fear the rich people in the church. You must not fear the poor people in the church. You must not fear the business community in the church. You must not fear the politicians in the church. You must not fear your wife. As soon as you are subject to any of these fears, you lose your authority and blessing in the ministry.

To fear men is to honour them above God. As soon as you do that, you will be demoted in the ministry. Jesus Christ did not fear the Pharisees. Jesus Christ did not fear his associate pastor. Jesus Christ did not fear rich people. He told them to sell all and follow Him. Indeed, Jesus Christ is the best example of a faithful shepherd who feared God and not men.

12. Disappointing shepherds do not delight in the things that please God.

...Has the LORD as much delight in burnt offerings and sacrifices as in obeying the voice of the LORD? Behold, to obey is better than sacrifice, And to heed than the fat of rams.

1 Samuel 15:22 (NASB)

This is because Sauline shepherds do not really know God. When you know someone, you will know what he likes and what he does not like. Almighty God obviously prefers obedience to all kinds of sacrifices we may want to make to Him. The bible teaches that we were created for His pleasure and we must live to please Him. Many people wear the clerical collar but do not know God. They do not know what God delights in.

13. Disappointing shepherds are rejected by God.

...Because you have rejected the word of the LORD, He has also rejected you from being king.

1 Samuel 15:23 (NASB)

Ultimately, pastors and shepherds with such qualities as I have described above will be rejected by God. You must strive so that your ministry will be accepted by God. God must be pleased with what you do otherwise there is no point in all you are doing.

Chapter 32

Twenty-Two Stages in the Development of a Shepherd

David the shepherd boy was anointed by Samuel and became the king of Israel. He was promoted from being the shepherd of a few sheep to becoming the famous shepherd of Israel. Psalm twenty-three reveals David's real life experience as a shepherd.

How did David become the anointed shepherd of Israel? It was through a long exacting process that lasted several years. From the moment he was chosen and anointed by Samuel, a journey began which ended on the throne of Israel.

In this chapter, I want to share with you the stages which David went through to become the renowned shepherd of Israel. These stages are important because they will be repeated in your own life as you also journey to become God's anointed servant. Learn these stages and follow the example of King David, who became the beloved of God and the sweet psalmist of Israel.

1. **Accept the sovereignty of God as revealed by your selection from among other brothers and sisters. David was selected from among his brethren and you will also be called out of your family.**

   Then Samuel took the horn of oil, and *anointed him in the midst of his brethren:* and the Spirit of the LORD came upon David from that day forward. So Samuel rose up, and went to Ramah.

   1 Samuel 16:13

2. **Develop a skill in the church like singing and playing instruments. David had developed the ability to play the harp and you must also learn such church-related skills.**

   Then answered one of the servants, and said, Behold, I have seen a son of Jesse the Bethlehemite, that is *cunning in playing, and a mighty valiant man*, and a man of war, and prudent in matters, and a comely person, and the LORD is with him.

1 Samuel 16:18

3. **Like David, become a spiritually mighty man by developing in prayer and the Word.**

Then answered one of the servants, and said, Behold, I have seen a son of Jesse the Bethlehemite, that is cunning in playing, and *a mighty valiant man, and a man of war*, and prudent in matters, and a comely person, and the LORD is with him.

1 Samuel 16:18

4. **Like David, demonstrate wisdom by listening to the advice of older more experienced people. This is something that young people do not often do.**

Then answered one of the servants, and said, Behold, I have seen a son of Jesse the Bethlehemite, that is cunning in playing, and a mighty valiant man, and a man of war, and *prudent in matters*, and a comely person, and the Lord is with him.

1 Samuel 16:18

5. **Become a servant of the existing minister, just as David became the armour bearer of Saul.**

And David came to Saul, and stood before him: and he loved him greatly; *and he became his armourbearer*.

1 Samuel 16:21

6. **Ensure that you find favour in the eyes of the one you serve. Some people lose favour when they work for the man of God.**

And David came to Saul, and stood before him: and *he loved him greatly*; and he became his armourbearer.

1 Samuel 16:21

7. **Become a well-known worker in the ministry just as David became a well-known court musician.**

And it came to pass, when the evil spirit from God was upon Saul, that *David took an harp, and played with his hand: so Saul was refreshed,* and was well, and the evil spirit departed from him.

1 Samuel 16:23

8. **Function as a shepherd by praying for the sheep, visiting the sheep, counselling them and interacting with them.**

And David rose up early in the morning, and left the sheep with a keeper, and took, and went, as Jesse had commanded him; and he came to the trench, as the host was going forth to the fight, and shouted for the battle.

1 Samuel 17:20

9. **Be brave and responsible by killing a bear and lion, just as David did.**

And David said unto Saul, Thy servant kept his father's sheep, and *there came a lion, and a bear, and took a lamb out of the flock: and I went out after him, and smote him*, and delivered it out of his mouth: and when he arose against me, I caught him by his beard, and smote him, and slew him.

1 Samuel 17:34-35

10. **Demonstrate that you understand your personal limitations. This is a quality that many do not have.**

And Saul armed David with his armour, and he put an helmet of brass upon his head; also he armed him with a coat of mail. And David girded his sword upon his armour, and he assayed to go; for he had not proved it. *And David said unto Saul, I cannot go with these;* for I have not proved them. And David put them off him. And he took his staff in his hand, and chose him five smooth stones out of the brook, and put them in a shepherd's bag which he had, even in a scrip; and his sling was in his hand: and he drew near to the Philistine.

1 Samuel 17:38-40

11. Demonstrate that you have learnt from your experiences by using what you are used to.

And he took his staff in his hand, and *chose him five smooth stones out of the brook*, and put them in a shepherd's bag which he had, even in a scrip; and his sling was in his hand: and he drew near to the Philistine.

1 Samuel 17:40

12. Manifest love and dedication for God and His people by killing Goliath in the name of the Lord.

Then said David to the Philistine, Thou comest to me with a sword, and with a spear, and with a shield: but I come to thee in the name of the LORD of hosts, *the God of the armies of Israel, whom thou hast defied*. This day will the LORD deliver thee into mine hand; and I will smite thee, and take thine head from thee; and I will give the carcases of the host of the Philistines this day unto the fowls of the air, and to the wild beasts of the earth; that all the earth may know that there is a God in Israel. And all this assembly shall know that the LORD saveth not with sword and spear: for the battle is the LORD's, and he will give you into our hands.

1 Samuel 17:45-47

13. Show evidence of your ability to develop intimate and close relationships with individuals and fellow ministers just as David developed a close relationship with Jonathan.

And it came to pass, when he had made an end of speaking unto Saul, that the soul of *Jonathan was knit with the soul of David, and Jonathan loved him as his own soul*. And Saul took him that day, and would let him go no more home to his father's house. Then Jonathan and David made a covenant, because he loved him as his own soul.

And Jonathan stripped himself of the robe that was upon him, and gave it to David, and his garments, even to his sword, and to his bow, and to his girdle.

1 Samuel 18:1-4

14. Show evidence of your ability to develop lifelong commitments with fellow workers just as David entered a lifelong covenant with Jonathan.

Then *Jonathan and David made a covenant*, because he loved him as his own soul.

1 Samuel 18:3

15. Show your ability to handle authority and promotion by behaving wisely when put in important positions.

And David went out whithersoever Saul sent him, and behaved himself wisely: and Saul set him over the men of war, and he was accepted in the sight of all the people, and also in the sight of Saul's servants.

1 Samuel 18:5

16. Gain a reputation among the congregation that will be useful in recommending you for ordination just as David did.

And it came to pass as they came, when David was returned from the slaughter of the Philistine, that the women came out of all cities of Israel, singing and dancing, to meet king Saul, with tabrets, with joy, and with instruments of musick. And the women answered one another as they played, and said, Saul hath slain his thousands, and David his ten thousands.

1 Samuel 18:6-7

17. Survive the jealousy of older ministers just as David did.

And it came to pass as they came, when David was returned from the slaughter of the Philistine, that the women came out of all cities of Israel, singing and dancing, to meet king Saul, with tabrets, with joy, and with instruments of musick.

And the women answered one another as they played, and said, Saul hath slain his thousands, and David his ten thousands. *And Saul was very wroth, and the saying displeased him; and he said, They have ascribed unto David ten thousands, and to me they have ascribed but thousands: and what can he have more but the kingdom? And Saul eyed David from that day and forward.*

1 Samuel 18:6-9

18. Survive the fierce anger of someone in authority over you just as David did.

And it came to pass on the morrow, that the evil spirit from God came upon Saul, and he prophesied in the midst of the house: and David played with his hand, as at other times: and there was a javelin in Saul's hand. *And Saul cast the javelin; for he said, I will smite David even to the wall with it. And David avoided out of his presence twice.*

1 Samuel 18:10-11

19. Survive attempts to remove you from your ministry just as David did.

And it came to pass on the morrow, that the evil spirit from God came upon Saul, and he prophesied in the midst of the house: and David played with his hand, as at other times: and there was a javelin in Saul's hand. *And Saul cast the javelin; for he said, I will smite David even to the wall with it. And David avoided out of his presence twice.*

1 Samuel 18:10-11

20. Display the highest kind of wisdom by avoiding men of God who tempt you to criticize them.

And Saul spake to Jonathan his son, and to all his servants, that they should kill David.

But Jonathan Saul's son delighted much in David: and Jonathan told David, saying, *Saul my father seeketh to kill thee: now therefore, I pray thee, take heed to thyself until the morning, and abide in a secret place, and hide thyself:*

1 Samuel 19:2

21. **Display the wisdom of running to safe places in the ministry for comfort, safety, anointing, direction and recovery just as David run to Samuel.**

So David fled, and escaped, and came to Samuel to Ramah, and told him all that Saul had done to him. And he and Samuel went and dwelt in Naioth. And it was told Saul, saying, Behold, David is at Naioth in Ramah. And Saul sent messengers to take David: and when they saw the company of the prophets prophesying, and Samuel standing as appointed over them, the Spirit of God was upon the messengers of Saul, and they also prophesied.

1 Samuel 19:18-20

22. **Accept the will of God to change your location just as David accepted to become a fugitive for many years.**

And it came to pass in the morning, that Jonathan went out into the field at the time appointed with David, and a little lad with him.

And he said unto his lad, Run, find out now the arrows which I shoot. And as the lad ran, he shot an arrow beyond him.

And when the lad was come to the place of the arrow which Jonathan had shot, Jonathan cried after the lad, and said, Is not the arrow beyond thee?

And Jonathan cried after the lad, Make speed, haste, stay not. And Jonathan's lad gathered up the arrows, and came to his master.

But the lad knew not any thing: only Jonathan and David knew the matter.

And Jonathan gave his artillery unto his lad, and said unto him, Go, carry them to the city.

And as soon as the lad was gone, David arose out of a place toward the south, and fell on his face to the ground, and bowed himself three times: and they kissed one another, and wept one with another, until David exceeded.

AND JONATHAN SAID TO DAVID, GO IN PEACE, FORASMUCH AS WE HAVE SWORN BOTH OF US IN THE NAME OF THE LORD, SAYING, THE LORD BE BETWEEN ME AND THEE, AND BETWEEN MY SEED AND THY SEED FOR EVER. And he arose and departed: and Jonathan went into the city.

1 Samuel 20:35-42

Chapter 33

How a Spiritual Son
Develops into a Shepherd

For this cause have I sent unto you Timotheus, who is my beloved son, and faithful in the Lord, who shall bring you into remembrance of my ways which be in Christ, as I teach every where in every church.
1 Corinthians 4:17

Timothy is the greatest example of a spiritual son who was transformed into a pastor. It is Timothy's sonship to Paul that gave Apostle Paul the authority and liberty to write to him the way he did. The apostle Paul freely told Timothy what to do and how to do it. When you are speaking to your own child, you feel free to say whatever is on your heart.

We are so blessed to have the book of first and second Timothy in which the apostle freely advises his spiritual son. Timothy's spiritual sonship opened him up to a high level of guidance and influence that flowed from the apostle. Timothy must have shown the apostle that he wanted to be fathered and taught. Timothy must also have encouraged the apostle Paul to teach him as much as he could. Timothy must have been eager to learn. This inspired Paul to counsel Timothy in great detail, even telling him what he should preach (2 Timothy 2:2).

There must have been other people that the apostle brought up whom he did not say all these things to. For instance, Diotrephes resisted the influence of the apostle John and John wrote about this in his third epistle: "I wrote unto the church: but Diotrephes, who loveth to have the preeminence among them, receiveth us not" (3 John 9).

When a minister no longer receives the word of the apostle, he opens himself up to judgement. Instead of receiving a new anointing, he receives judgement: "He that rejecteth me, and receiveth not my words, hath one that judgeth him: the word that I have spoken, the same shall judge him in the last day" (John 12:48).

It is important that you demonstrate important characteristics of sonship. This will open you up to the blessings of a father. It will stir up the anointing and provoke the gift of the apostle on your behalf. Develop the signs that demonstrate sonship. They will open you up to amazing blessings.

1. You must demonstrate the teachable spirit of a son.

When you are teachable, you will be taught many things that you did not know. A teacher always senses the presence of a "know-it-all". Teachers always recognize resistance and unwillingness to learn.

But continue thou in THE THINGS WHICH THOU HAST LEARNED and hast been assured of, knowing of whom thou hast learned them;

2 Timothy 3:14

2. You must demonstrate the flowing attitude of a son.

For I have NO MAN LIKEMINDED, who will naturally care for your state.

Philippians 2:20

The word "flowing" means ten different things:

1. A flowing son has a *kindred* spirit.
2. A flowing son has a *similar* attitude to his spiritual father. If the father loves soul winning he also loves soul winning.
3. A flowing son is *like-minded*.
4. A flowing son is *compatible* with his father.
5. A flowing son *understands* his father's problems.
6. A flowing son is *sympathetic* to his father's issues.
7. A flowing son is *agreeable and not contentious or full of debate*.

8. A flowing son is *in tune* with the vision and ideas of his father.

9. A flowing son is *friendly and relational.*

10. A flowing son is *companionable*. This means that he can be a companion with you on your journey. Some people are not good company. They have nothing to say about anything. All their thoughts are within.

3. **You must demonstrate the caring attitude of a true son.** A son's eyes are full of love and care for his father.

   For I have no man likeminded, WHO WILL NATURALLY CARE for your state.

   Philippians 2:20

4. **You must demonstrate the servant attitude of a son.**

   For all seek their own, not the things which are Jesus Christ's. But ye know the proof of him, that, as a son with the father, HE HATH SERVED WITH ME in the gospel.

   Philippians 2:21-22

5. **You must demonstrate the loyalty of a son.** A son is faithful even in difficult times. It is your faithfulness in difficult times that proves your sonship.

   For all seek their own, not the things which are Jesus Christ's. But ye know the proof of him, that, AS A SON WITH THE FATHER, he hath served with me in the gospel.

   Philippians 2:21-22

6. **You must demonstrate the ability to pass the tests that prove you are a son.** As time goes by, there are different situations that will come to prove whether you are a true son. You will be tested on your ability to be open, humble and yielding. You will also be tested on your ability to follow until the very end.

For all seek their own, not the things which are Jesus Christ's. **BUT YE KNOW THE PROOF OF HIM, that, as a son with the father, he hath served with me in the gospel.**

Philippians 2:21-22

7. **You must demonstrate the childlike attitude of a son.** A child is very trusting whilst grown-ups are wary and suspicious.

For all seek their own, not the things which are Jesus Christ's. But ye know the proof of him, that, **AS A SON WITH THE FATHER,** he hath served with me in the gospel.

Philippians 2:21-22

8. **You must demonstrate your sonship by ensuring that your father's work is continued.**

AND SENT TIMOTHEUS, OUR BROTHER, and minister of God, and our fellowlabourer in the gospel of Christ, TO ESTABLISH YOU, and to comfort you concerning your faith:

1 Thessalonians 3:2

A spiritual son ensures that what his father has started is established. Paul went to great lengths to establish churches. He travelled all over the known world to win lost souls and to build churches. His spiritual son was prepared to go to the same extent to establish his father's work. A true son would want to see that whatever his father has started continues to grow. Those who are not true sons could not care less about what happens to the vision and life's work of their father. Notice how Timothy went forth to establish what Paul had began.

9. **You must demonstrate your sonship by ensuring that the words of your father are kept and obeyed.** After a founder or father is gone, there are always people who try to change what he said and did. A true son fights for the doctrines and

philosophies of his father to be established. His main concern is not to also write a book but to ensure that the books that have been written are taught and understood.

As I besought thee to abide still at Ephesus, when I went into Macedonia, that THOU MIGHTEST CHARGE SOME THAT THEY TEACH NO OTHER DOCTRINE,

1 Timothy 1:3

And the things that thou hast heard of me among many witnesses, THE SAME COMMIT THOU TO FAITHFUL MEN, who shall be able to teach others also.

2 Timothy 2:2

10. **You must demonstrate your sonship by having the same level of zeal as your father.** Titus was asked to preach with the same passion, emphasis and authority. A person who is not a son will not speak on the same subject as his father nor will he say those things with the same passion and authority as his father. People who are not true sons will speak on other subjects with authority.

THESE THINGS SPEAK, and exhort, and rebuke with all authority. Let no man despise thee.

Titus 2:15

Chapter 34

Core Areas for the Development of a Shepherd

1. SHEPHERDS MUST DEVELOP THE ABILITY TO FIGHT.

Ministry is honourable service to God. However, being in the ministry also implies the reality of serving in a military campaign. Ministry is the same as being at war. You become a target of an enemy who hates you. You become the subject of discussion of wicked spirits whose one goal is to extinguish your light. You must learn to fight and to fight well. Do not give up or retreat at all! Warfare is so important that I have written a whole book on the subject.

> **This charge I commit unto thee, son Timothy, according to the prophecies which went before on thee, that thou by them mightest war a good warfare;**
>
> **1 Timothy 1:18**

2. SHEPHERDS MUST DEVELOP THEIR CONSCIENCE.

> **Now the end of the commandment is charity out of a pure heart, and of a good conscience, and of faith unfeigned:**
>
> **1 Timothy 1:5**

The conscience is the still small voice that speaks from within warning you about right and wrong. Whether the conscience is the voice of the spirit or the voice of the soul, I cannot really tell. But what I do know is that it is the warning light from "within" that lets you know when you are doing something wrong.

Having a good conscience is like having a sensitive warning system deep within. If you set aside this warning system, you will expose yourself to untold dangers.

The recent tsunami in Asia took the world by surprise and left hundreds of thousands dead. The reason for the massive death toll was the absence of a deep sea warning system. Since the tsunami, they have developed special warning systems deep within the sea that can pick up danger signs and transmit warnings to offices thousands of miles away.

This tsunami warning system is expected to help in the event of another massive earthquake. In the case of the tsunami, it is easy to see how many people could have escaped if they had had five minutes of warning. That is why God put our consciences in us; so we could be warned by the Holy Spirit.

Like the tsunami warning system, the conscience can be more or less sensitive. The more sensitive it is, the more you will find yourself confessing your sins and praying for mercy every few minutes. The less sensitive the warning system, the fewer things you will confess.

If you have a seared or hardened conscience, you will not confess your sins often. If you have a hardened conscience, you will see yourself as righteous. Repeated sin also leads to a hardened conscience. "Because sentence against an evil work is not executed speedily, therefore the heart of the sons of men is fully set in them to do evil" (Ecclesiastes 8:11).

Holding faith, and a good conscience; which some having put away concerning faith have made shipwreck: of whom is Hymenaeus and Alexander; whom I have delivered unto Satan, that they may learn not to blaspheme.

1 Timothy 1:19-20

As you can see from the Scripture above, Hymenaeus and Alexander put aside a good conscience and made shipwreck of their faith. Setting aside a sensitive warning system is a dangerous thing to do. You must be careful to maintain a good conscience all your life. It is better to be over-apologetic than to be over-righteous. "Be not righteous over much; neither make thyself over wise: why shouldest thou destroy thyself?" (Ecclesiastes 7:16).

3. SHEPHERDS MUST DEVELOP GODLINESS.

But thou, O man of God, flee these things; and follow after righteousness, godliness, faith, love, patience, meekness.

1 Timothy 6:11

Pastors must develop themselves to become more like God. Jehovah embodies beautiful spiritual characteristics such as righteousness, holiness, faith, love, patience and meekness. These qualities do not sound very powerful or even attractive. But they are the most important things that must develop in your spiritual lives.

God is actually at work in us to transform us into the image of His Son. Our destiny is not success and fame. *Our destiny is to develop into the image of God.* Read your Bible carefully and discover your predestined destiny. "For whom he did foreknow, he also did predestinate to be conformed to the image of his Son, that he might be the firstborn among many brethren" (Romans 8:29).

4. SHEPHERDS MUST HAVE SPIRITUAL PURSUITS.

But flee from these things, you man of God, and pursue righteousness, godliness, faith, love, perseverance and gentleness.

1 Timothy 6:11 (NASB)

The word "pursue" is translated from the Greek word dioko. This word is translated "pursue" and speaks of giving yourself to something and following hard after it.

Most pastors have physical or natural goals. Our prayer topics reveal this reality. We rarely pray for spiritual things like humility, love and holiness. We often pray for tangible things like money or growth in numbers. You will notice that the apostle Paul rather prayed for spiritual things such as the spirit of wisdom and revelation (Ephesians 1:17). He prayed that they would know the love of God (Ephesians 3:18). These apparently abstract topics are the most important things. They yield far greater dividends and are far more relevant than you realize.

As I have grown up in the Lord, I have found myself praying more and more for these kinds of things. I did not pray for such spiritual things at the beginning of my Christian life and ministry. Now, I sense my desperate need for these spiritual things. Indeed, you may think that pastors would naturally pursue spiritual things. On the contrary, our carnality is revealed in our pursuits and our pursuits are revealed in our prayer.

5. SHEPHERDS MUST DEVELOP THEIR GIFTS.

Gifted people are seen as men who have a special grace on their lives. This may be true but usually, the most "gifted" people are those who work hardest. They practice more, they prepare more and they invest more into the area of their gifting. A close-up analysis of an apparently gifted person will always lead you to a difficult question. *"Is this person really gifted or does he just work very hard?"*

If you go into the lives of gifted pianists, golfers, soccer players, etc., you will discover the long hours and hard work that go to make them what they are. This is why the Scripture teaches us to develop our gifts.

You would have thought that once you were gifted, no more work would be needed. On the contrary, your gift is the reason why you must work hard.

Give yourself wholly to the development of your gift. Work hard and invest in the gifts that God has given you.

Neglect not the gift that is in thee, which was given thee by prophecy, with the laying on of the hands of the presbytery. Meditate upon these things; give thyself wholly to them; that thy profiting may appear to all.

1 Timothy 4:14-15

6. SHEPHERDS MUST DEVELOP LOYALTY.

Pastoral work has to do with leading people and guiding them into God's will. People have a tendency to become disloyal. The evil spirits in the atmosphere constantly influence people to be rebel against God and His servants. Sadly, many ministers do not have an understanding of this all-important subject.

You will never build a large ministry unless you have a lot of loyal people helping you. The understanding of loyalty must be deepened. The principles that govern human behaviour and the creation of a loyal following must be studied in earnest. You must have at least, a superficial knowledge of these principles. Simply frightening people with warnings about disloyalty will not make people loyal. Raining curses on people if they dare to be disloyal will also not make your followers loyal.

A basic characteristic of the devil is a fearless lack of respect. Satan has no respect for authority. The spirit of rebellion does not care who you are or what rank you have. It fearlessly challenges authority and inspires traitors to rise against the highest kinds of leaders.

You must study loyalty and become a loyal person yourself! You must develop styles of leadership that engender loyalty! You must develop teachings that introduce knowledge about loyalty and warn about disloyalty!

O Timothy, keep that which is committed to thy trust, avoiding profane and vain babblings, and oppositions of science falsely so called:

1 Timothy 6:20

7. PASTORS MUST DEVELOP THE ABILITY TO BE EXAMPLES.

Being an example to your flock is as important as teaching them the word of God. Actually, people learn more from the example you set than from the teachings you give them.

A pastor's life is under constant scrutiny. His marriage is observed by the church members. His home is assessed by the people. The car he drives is of great interest to many. Many people ask the questions, "What kind of car does he drive? Where does he live? What does he eat? Who are his friends? Where does he get money from? Where is he?"

Let no man despise thy youth; but be thou an example of the believers, in word, in conversation, in charity, in spirit, in faith, in purity.

1 Timothy 4:12

There are two unspoken reasons for this kind of scrutiny. The first reason is that many are looking for the opportunity to criticise a bad example set by the pastor. The other reason is that many people want to follow him.

You would be surprised at how many people follow the dressing, hairstyles, type of car and other minor aspects of a pastor's life. Poor people look at the example of the pastor to see if their kind is accepted in the church. Rich people equally look at the example of the pastor to see if rich people are welcome.

Develop the art of being a good example. You must accept that your pastoral calling will limit you for the rest of your life. You will not be able to do certain things if you want to be a good example. Always remember that the art of being a good example is different from your teaching ministry, which lays out principles for the sheep to follow.

The example of Christ in which He took His cross and laid down His life says much more than His teachings "For even hereunto were ye called: because Christ also suffered for us, leaving us an example, that ye should follow his steps" (1 Peter 2:21). That sacrificial example has inspired and directed many people to do the same.

8. PASTORS MUST DEVELOP AN ALL-OUT ATTITUDE.

Till I come, give attendance to reading, to exhortation, to doctrine. Neglect not the gift that is in thee, which

was given thee by prophecy, with the laying on of the hands of the presbytery. Meditate upon these things; GIVE THYSELF WHOLLY TO THEM; that thy profiting may appear to all.

1 Timothy 4:13-15

Giving yourself wholly to your ministry is as important as being called. There are some things that do not work unless you do them in an "all-out" way.

My ministry was transformed dramatically when I gave myself wholly to it. I recommend that you give yourself wholly to the work of the church.

If you are a pastor who travels away from your church most of the time, you are not giving yourself wholly to your pastoral ministry. You are actually a part-time pastor.

If you do not feed your congregation regularly, you are not giving yourself wholly to your pastoral ministry. It is time to give yourself completely to your calling. Throw yourself into it. Go all out. You will see great improvements in your ministry.

Chapter 35

How a Young Person Can Become a Shepherd

Let no man despise thy youth; but be thou an example of the believers, in word, in conversation, in charity, in spirit, in faith, in purity.

1 Timothy 4:12

Pastors must develop confidence in spite of being young. Your youthfulness could be your greatest advantage in the ministry. But it is often seen as a great handicap. There are many reasons why youthfulness is despised and the following are just a few.

Six Reasons Why Young People Are Despised

1. **Youthful people sense strong sexual urges which constantly remind them of their lack of holiness.** The mysterious world of sexuality plus the desire to discover it, is a major source of confusion to young people. This feeling removes their confidence in the things of God.

   The constant sexual desires, erections, dreams, wet dreams, sexual encounters, plus the interest in pornographic material, films, romantic books, etc., all serve to remove the confidence of a young person. This is why young people easily despise themselves and allow others to despise them.

2. **The fear of failure is a great source of confusion to the young person.** These fears are fuelled by the young person's lack of knowledge, lack of experience and worst of all, his youthful desires. Fears can lead a young person away from his calling. It can cause him to stay away from the purposes of God.

3. **Young people are aware of their lack of knowledge.** Obviously, you will acquire more knowledge as you grow

older. The young person may be keenly aware of the fact that
he does not know many things.

4. **Young people know that they lack experience.** After
discovering that life does not proceed down a logical pathway,
young people who have a bit of wisdom become aware of
their lack of experience. They then tend to look up to people
who have experience. The devil whispers, "You have never
done it before" , "You have never seen it before."

5. **Young people lack maturity.** Maturity grows out of a
combination of knowledge and experience. There is a certain
mellowness, which comes to a man who has both knowledge
and experience. His decisions are tempered by both "the
facts" and history. A young person often knows that he lacks
the advantage of these two things.

6. **Young people are full of unbridled zeal.** They may
champion causes which the mature man would not touch.
They pursue causes that the mature person knows will never
succeed. The mature person looks on the zealous young man
who takes on ancient problems that have not been solved by
better people. Youthful people are seen as people with great
passion but without experience.

It is for these reasons that Paul asked the young pastor,
Timothy, not to allow anyone to despise his youthfulness.

Seven Reasons Why Young People Are Useful in Ministry

There are also reasons why young people are especially useful
in the ministry.

1. **Young people are special and useful because Jesus Christ
was a young person when He started His ministry.**
Timothy was also a young person, but was used greatly by
the Lord.

2. **Young people are useful in the ministry because they have a lot of zeal.** Older people are usually tired and discouraged about many things.

3. **Young people are particularly useful because they have more faith in the Word of God and in the man of God.** Our lives and ministry are dependent on our faith. Without faith it is impossible to please Him.

4. **Young people are useful because their sexual drive is actually a symptom of the strength needed to do the work of the Lord.** Usually, the absence of a sexual drive reveals the absence of a drive in other areas. The sexual desires and urges, though frightening, are actually a symptom of something good.

5. **Young people are especially useful because they do not have many financial problems.** The cares of the world are much fewer when you are young. The responsibilities that people have in life really weigh them down and turn them into weary tired souls.

6. **Young people are especially useful because they do not have children to look after.** Bringing up children places many demands on parents. Young people discover that their lives take a dramatic downturn in fruitfulness when they have children.

7. **Young people are particularly useful to God because they will have enough time to begin and complete God's commandments for their lives.** True ministry often takes up your whole life. Even a life of seventy years is not enough to accomplish much. How much do you think you can accomplish if you start your ministry when you are fifty? Young people are able to do so much more for God because they start out early.

Seven Ways for Young People to Develop Confidence

1. **Young people can gain confidence by reading a lot.** Knowledge comes by reading.

   Till I come, give attendance to reading, to exhortation, to doctrine.

   1 Timothy 4:13

2. **Young people can develop confidence by listening to CDs and watching videos.**

3. **Young people can become wise by studying history.** They can gain all the experiential knowledge by studying history. Older people who do not study history can be equally limited because their personal experiences are always limited.

4. **Young people can develop confidence by praying for wisdom.**

5. **Young people can develop confidence by learning from older experienced fathers.**

6. **Young people can develop confidence by surrounding themselves with wise counsellors.**

7. **Young people can develop confidence from the mistakes of the people just ahead of them.** The mistakes of someone just ahead of you reveals the location of pitfalls. They will show you what to avoid in future.

Section 3

THE SHEPHERD'S HEART

Chapter 36

The Heart as the Centre of Your Ministry

The human heart is a large pumping machine situated in the centre of the body. We know that the heart is basically a pump. But we also know that the heart is at the centre of the human body. The word "heart' is translated from the Hebrew word *labab* and emphasizes the fact that the heart is in the central part of the body.

The Scripture focuses more on the fact that the heart is the "innermost core" of a person rather than the fact that it is a pump. That is why the word "heart" is used in expressions like "the heart of the sea", "the heart of heaven", "the heart of a tree" and "the heart of the earth".

What is the Centre of Your Ministry?

1. The *choicest part* of something.

2. The *most essential part* of an object.

3. The *most vital part* of some idea or experience.

4. The object upon which *interest and attention focuses*.

5. The centre of a thing speaks of *the foundation of a thing*.

6. A place where some particular *activity is concentrated*.

7. The *middle of a military or naval* formation.

8. The *spiritual hub* of your life.

9. The *focal point* around which events evolve.

10. The *nucleus* around which things rotate.

This is why the heart is so important. We all know that foundations determine the eventual outcome. This is why the outcome of somebody's ministry is determined by his heart.

Because of our human nature, we tend to overlook the heart and make assessments by outward things. But outward aspects determine far less than the hidden heart of the man. The centre of every man's life and ministry is his heart. It is out of the centre of a thing that the issues arise.

That is why many capital cities of the world are located in the centre of their countries. For example, Rome, Madrid, Tokyo, Bogota, Brasilia and Abuja are roughly in the centre of their respective countries. A country's destiny is often determined from its centre. Several Scriptures bring out the revelation about the *heart* of a thing being the *centre* around which it revolves.

1. The heart of the sea. This speaks of the innermost and deepest part of the sea.

    And with the blast of thy nostrils the waters were gathered together, the floods stood upright as an heap, and the depths were congealed IN THE HEART (*labab*) OF THE SEA.

    Exodus 15:8

2. The midst of Heaven. This speaks of the innermost, secret and intimate part of Heaven.

    And ye came near and stood under the mountain; and the mountain burned with fire unto THE MIDST (*labab*) OF HEAVEN, with darkness, clouds, and thick darkness.

    Deuteronomy 4:11

3. The midst of the oak. This speaks of the core and nucleus of the tree.

    Then said Joab, I may not tarry thus with thee. And he took three darts in his hand, and thrust them through the heart of Absalom, while he was yet alive in THE MIDST (*labab*) OF THE OAK.

    2 Samuel 18:14

4. The heart of the earth. This speaks of the innermost and deepest part of the earth.

For as Jonas was three days and three nights in the whale's belly; so shall the Son of man be three days and three nights in THE HEART (*labab*) OF THE EARTH.

Matthew 12:40

5. The heart of your life is the centre of your life.

And the peace of God, which passeth all understanding, shall keep your HEARTS and minds through Christ Jesus.

Philippians 4:7 (KJV)

Before you know it, a sense of God's wholeness, everything coming together for good, will come and settle you down. It's wonderful what happens when Christ displaces worry AT THE CENTER OF YOUR LIFE.

Philippians 4:7 (The Message Bible)

Perhaps you can now understand why the Bible teaches us to guard our hearts with all diligence. If the heart is the most important part of a thing, it is no wonder it has to be guarded so zealously. "Keep thy heart with all diligence; for out of it are the issues of life" (Proverbs 4:23).

Chapter 37

How You Can Understand the Spiritual Heart by Comparing It with the Human Heart

1. **The human heart is located in the centre of the breast.**
   This shows us that the spiritual heart is located in the centre of
   a person's thoughts, words, actions and ministry. A person's
   heart is the very foundation of his ministry. That is why the
   heart is so important. Everything that a person achieves
   depends on his heart. Everything you become depends on
   your heart.

2. **The human heart is about as big as your clenched fist.** In
   other words, your heart is as big as your hand. What does
   this mean? It shows that the works of your hands will only
   be as big as your heart. The larger your heart, the larger your
   hand. **If you have a bigger heart, you will be able to do
   greater works with your hand.** It is time for you to allow
   God to work on your heart so that you can do greater works.
   The "largeness" of somebody's ministry is determined by the
   "largeness" of his heart.

3. **The human heart contains blood, which contains all the
   nutrients.** These nutrients come from what you have eaten.
   This shows us that your heart is affected by what you take
   in. **The contents of your spiritual heart are made up of
   what you have heard and received.** Many things enter your
   heart after they have been in your mind for a while. You must
   allow good things to come into your heart. You must also
   prevent evil things from coming into your heart.

4. **The human heart works by receiving and then giving
   blood.** This fact demonstrates how a person's life is affected
   by the heart. It is the blood that is received into the heart
   that is pumped out. A person receives blood into his heart
   and pumps out fresh life-giving blood to the rest of the body.

This means that what you allow to come into your heart is what you eventually give out.

5. **The human heart pumps blood to the furthermost and distant parts of the body.** This demonstrates how the spiritual heart affects the furthermost and minutest aspects of your life. **Every little aspect of your life is somehow affected by what is in your heart.** This is why the heart is so important, because it affects everything about you.

6. **The human heart gives life to the whole body by pumping oxygenated blood to all parts of the body.** This shows us that the heart of a person is what releases life, joy and peace. The life-giving part of your ministry is your heart.

7. **When the content of the human heart is contaminated, the contamination is pumped out to affect the entire body.** Likewise, when the spiritual heart is polluted with any form of evil, this defilement is pumped to the rest of the body. Bitterness is a good example of something evil that can enter the heart. It is easy to see a person whose heart is filled with bitterness and unforgiveness. His heart pumps out that bitterness into the rest of his ministry and this is evident to the discerning eye. When he speaks, you sense the bitterness. When he preaches it just comes out. Be careful of what you allow to enter your heart.

8. **The human heart gets sick when it has a high fat diet.** This shows us that the heart of a pastor gets sick when he receives too many messages on riches. The Body of Christ has developed heart problems through the abundance of prosperity teachings.

9. **The human heart is more prone to disease in a body that gets little exercise.** This truth shows us how the spiritual heart gets sick when it has received a lot of good feeding of the Word but has not put it into practice. Likewise, the spiritual heart is more prone to disease in a person with little chance to practise what he knows. The lack of missionary work, a lack of evangelism and a lack of outreach have caused heart problems in the body of Christ.

10. **The human heart is more prone to disease in a body that takes in alcohol.** Likewise, the spiritual heart is affected by intoxicants like the pleasures of this world which multiply deceptions and delusions in our lives.

Chapter 38

Why the Shepherd's Heart Is Important

Keep thy heart with all diligence; for OUT OF IT ARE THE ISSUES OF LIFE.

Proverbs 4:23 (KJV)

1. **The pastor's heart is important because of the strong admonition to guard it.** Anything that is heavily guarded is important. The extent of security around a building reveals how sensitive and important it is. The strong admonition in the Bible to protect the heart reveals how important it is.

    KEEP THY HEART with all diligence; for out of it are the issues of life.

    Proverbs 4:23 (KJV)

    Above all else, GUARD YOUR AFFECTIONS. For they influence everything else in your life.

    Proverbs 4:23 (TLB)

2. **The pastor's heart is important because it is the source of all that he ministers.**

    Keep thy heart with all diligence; for OUT OF IT ARE THE ISSUES OF LIFE.

    Proverbs 4:23

3. **The pastor's heart is important because it is the source of all issues and problems.** Most of the problems that we have emanate from the heart. This is why problems must be solved at the heart level. Often, problems are solved superficially without dealing with the heart. That is why the problems continue endlessly.

    Keep thy heart with all diligence; for OUT OF IT ARE THE ISSUES OF LIFE.

    Proverbs 4:23

4. **The pastor's heart is important because it influences everything in his life.**

   Above all else, guard your affections. FOR THEY INFLUENCE EVERYTHING ELSE IN YOUR LIFE.
   Proverbs 4:23 (TLB)

5. **The pastor's heart is important because that is where life begins.** If your ministry is full of life it is because your heart is full of life.

   Keep vigilant watch over your heart; THAT'S WHERE LIFE STARTS.
   Proverbs 4:23 (The Message Bible)

6. **The pastor's heart is important because it is an "unknowable" element.** We do not even know our own hearts. It is difficult to know what is in your own heart. How important it is to search your heart until you are sure of what is in it! Could there be evil things in my heart that are working themselves out and affecting me negatively?

   The heart is deceitful above all things, and desperately wicked: WHO CAN KNOW IT?
   Jeremiah 17:9

   Search me, O God, and KNOW MY HEART: TRY ME, and know my thoughts:
   Psalm 139:23

7. **The pastor's heart is important because it is a treasure box containing many good things.** A treasure is a collection of valuable and sometimes old objects. The heart has a collection of valuable, important things that have been there for a long time. The heart is hidden from our view even though it contains many valuable things. Such is the heart of a pastor. It contains the valuable ingredients that can make or break him.

A good man out of the GOOD TREASURE OF THE HEART bringeth forth good things: and an evil man out of the evil treasure bringeth forth evil things.

Matthew 12:35

8. **The pastor's heart is important because it is also a source of many evil things.** The heart is the source of both good things and evil things. The evil that men do emanates from their very hearts. When the heart is saved and changed, the evil stream is stemmed.

For from within, OUT OF THE HEART OF MEN, PROCEED evil thoughts, adulteries, fornications, murders, thefts, covetousness, wickedness, deceit, lasciviousness, an evil eye, blasphemy, pride, foolishness: all these evil things come from within, and defile the man.

Mark 7:21-23

9. **The pastor's heart is important because it can be a residence for God.** God has chosen to dwell in our hearts. This makes the heart important. If God is with you, He is in your heart. If God speaks to you, He speaks to your heart. This makes your heart a very important place. Open your heart to Jesus. Ensure that no one else is in your heart. Ensure that nothing else apart from Christ is in your heart.

THAT CHRIST MAY DWELL IN YOUR HEARTS by faith; that ye, being rooted and grounded in love,

Ephesians 3:17

Behold, I stand at the door, and knock: if any man hear my voice, and open the door, I will come in to him, and will sup with him, and he with me.

Revelation 3:20

10. **The pastor's heart is important because it can be a residence for demons.** The heart can also be a residence for evil spirits. Once again, this makes the heart very important.

When the unclean spirit is gone out of a man, he walketh through dry places, seeking rest, and findeth none. Then he saith, I will return into my house from whence I came out; and when he is come, he findeth it empty, swept, and garnished. Then goeth he, AND TAKETH WITH HIMSELF SEVEN OTHER SPIRITS MORE WICKED THAN HIMSELF, AND THEY ENTER IN and dwell there: and the last state of that man is worse than the first. Even so shall it be also unto this wicked generation.

Matthew 12:43-45

Chapter 39

Develop Flowing Hearts

The Bible describes different kinds of hearts. It is important to work on your heart so that you develop the right kind of heart. Without the right kind of heart you cannot accomplish much for the Lord. Because the heart is at the centre of your ministry, it will determine the outcome of everything you do.

1. **Develop a willing heart. A willing heart is a heart that is inclined to yield itself to a thing.**

   Speak unto the children of Israel, that they bring me an offering: of every man that GIVETH IT WILLINGLY WITH HIS HEART ye shall take my offering.

   Exodus 25:2

2. **Develop a stirred heart. A stirred heart is a heart that is excited and moved toward the expression of an emotion.**

   And they came, EVERY ONE WHOSE HEART STIRRED HIM UP, and every one whom his spirit made willing, and they brought the Lord's offering to the work of the tabernacle of the congregation, and for all his service, and for the holy garments.

   Exodus 35:21

3. **Develop a soft heart. A soft heart is a heart that is compassionate and kind. A soft heart is a conciliatory heart.**

   For God maketh MY HEART SOFT, and the Almighty troubleth me:

   Job 23:16

4. **Develop a communing heart. A communing heart is a heart that you can communicate intimately with. It is a heart that is in a state of heightened intimate receptivity to God.**

Stand in awe, and sin not: COMMUNE WITH YOUR OWN HEART upon your bed, and be still. Selah.

Psalms 4:4

5. **Develop a heart of wax. A heart of wax is a pliable heart. It is also a heart that has assumed a specified characteristic, quality or state.**

I am poured out like water, and all my bones are out of joint: MY HEART IS LIKE WAX; it is melted in the midst of my bowels.

Psalms 22:14

6. **Develop a burning heart. A burning heart is a heart that experiences a strong emotion or desire.**

Then he said unto them, O fools, and slow of heart to believe all that the prophets have spoken: Ought not Christ to have suffered these things, and to enter into his glory? And beginning at Moses and all the prophets, he expounded unto them in all the scriptures the things concerning himself. And they drew nigh unto the village, whither they went: and he made as though he would have gone further. But they constrained him, saying, Abide with us: for it is toward evening, and the day is far spent. And he went in to tarry with them. And it came to pass, as he sat at meat with them, he took bread, and blessed it, and brake, and gave to them. And their eyes were opened, and they knew him; and he vanished out of their sight. And they said one to another, DID NOT OUR HEART BURN WITHIN US, while he talked with us by the way, and while he opened to us the scriptures?

Luke 24:25-32

7. **Develop one heart with those called of God. This is a heart that is in agreement with and united with the brethren.**

And the multitude of THEM THAT BELIEVED WERE OF ONE HEART and of one soul: neither said any of them

that ought of the things which he possessed was his own;
but they had all things common.

Acts 4:32

8. Develop an opened heart. An opened heart is a heart that allows God access. It is a heart that is not protected, fastened or sealed. This type of heart is willing and ready to consider. It is a heart that is available and ready for use by God.

And a certain woman named Lydia, a seller of purple, of
the city of Thyatira, which worshipped God, heard us:
WHOSE HEART THE LORD OPENED, that she attended
unto the things which were spoken of Paul.

Acts 16:14

9. Develop an obedient heart. An obedient heart is a heart that dutifully complies with the commands and instructions of God. It is a heart that is submissive to the authority and will of the Father.

But God be thanked, that ye were the servants of sin, BUT
YE HAVE OBEYED FROM THE HEART that form of
doctrine which was delivered you.

Romans 6:17

10. Develop a steadfast heart. A steadfast heart is a heart that is firmly fixed, steady and immovable. It is a loyal, unwavering heart.

NEVERTHELESS HE THAT STANDETH STEDFAST
IN HIS HEART, having no necessity, but hath power over
his own will, and hath so decreed in his heart that he will
keep his virgin, doeth well.

1 Corinthians 7:37

Chapter 40

Avoid an
Unyielding Heart

The Bible also describes different kinds of stubborn hearts. It is important to work on your heart so that you avoid having an unyielding heart. Without the right kind of heart you cannot accomplish much for the Lord. Because the heart is the centre of your ministry, it will determine the outcome of everything you do. You must really avoid having an unyielding heart. As you will discover, unyielding hearts are some of the ugliest hearts you can ever have.

1. **Avoid a hardened heart. A hardened heart is a dispassionate heart that is not easily penetrated. A hardened heart does not yield even under pressure.**

   And the LORD said unto Moses, When thou goest to return into Egypt, see that thou do all those wonders before Pharaoh, which I have put in thine hand: BUT I WILL HARDEN HIS HEART, that he shall not let the people go.

   Exodus 4:21

2. **Avoid a rebellious heart. A rebellious heart is a heart that tends to defy, resist and oppose control and authority.**

   BUT THIS PEOPLE HATH A REVOLTING AND A REBELLIOUS HEART; they are revolted and gone.

   Jeremiah 5:23

3. **Avoid a stony heart. A stony heart is a cold and unresponsive heart that demonstrates an unfeeling resistance to external influences. A stony heart has no tender feelings.**

   And I will give them one heart, and I will put a new spirit within you; AND I WILL TAKE THE STONY HEART

OUT OF THEIR FLESH, and will give them an heart of flesh:

Ezekiel 11:19

4. **Avoid a proud heart. A proud heart is a haughty and conceited heart.**

Whoso privily slandereth his neighbour, him will I cut off: HIM THAT HATH AN HIGH LOOK AND A PROUD HEART WILL NOT I SUFFER.

Psalms 101:5

5. **Avoid a darkened heart. A darkened heart is one that lacks enlightenment, knowledge or culture. It is a sinister and evil heart.**

Because that, when they knew God, they glorified him not as God, neither were thankful; but became vain in their imaginations, and THEIR FOOLISH HEART WAS DARKENED.

Romans 1:21

6. **Avoid an unbelieving heart. An unbelieving heart is a heart that is sceptical and questioning.**

Take heed, brethren, LEST THERE BE IN ANY OF YOU AN EVIL HEART OF UNBELIEF, in departing from the living God.

Hebrews 3:12

Chapter 41

Develop a
Healthy Heart

The Bible describes different kinds of hearts. It is important to work on your heart so that you develop a healthy heart. Without the right kind of heart you cannot accomplish much for the Lord. Because the heart is at the centre of your ministry, it will determine the outcome of everything you do.

1. **Develop a forgiving heart. A forgiving heart is a heart that is able to show mercy.**

   So likewise shall my heavenly Father do also unto you, IF YE FROM YOUR HEARTS FORGIVE NOT every one his brother their trespasses.

   Matthew 18:35

2. **Develop a pure heart. A pure heart is a heart that is free from anything that corrupts. It is a clean and chaste heart that is free from anything that contaminates.**

   HE THAT HATH CLEAN HANDS, AND A PURE HEART; who hath not lifted up his soul unto vanity, nor sworn deceitfully.

   Psalms 24:4

3. **Develop a perfect heart. A perfect heart is a heart that is entirely without fault, defect or blemish.**

   All these men of war, that could keep rank, CAME WITH A PERFECT HEART to Hebron, to make David king over all Israel: and all the rest also of Israel were of one heart to make David king.

   1 Chronicles 12:38

4. **Develop an upright heart. An upright heart is characterized by strong moral correctness. It is an honest and honourable heart.**

MY WORDS SHALL BE OF THE UPRIGHTNESS OF MY HEART: and my lips shall utter knowledge clearly.

Job 33:3

5. **Develop a living heart. A living heart is heart that is alive and still in active use.**

The humble shall see this, and be glad: and YOUR HEART SHALL LIVE that seek God.

Psalms 69:32

6. **Develop a sound heart. A sound heart is a heart that is in a good condition; free from flaw, defect or damage.**

A SOUND HEART IS THE LIFE OF THE FLESH: but envy the rottenness of the bones.

Proverbs 14:30

7. **Develop a new heart. A new heart is a heart that has just come into being by the power of God. It is a fresh heart that is brought to replace the old one with its old ways.**

Therefore I will judge you, O house of Israel, every one according to his ways, saith the Lord GOD. Repent, and turn yourselves from all your transgressions; so iniquity shall not be your ruin.

Cast away from you all your transgressions, whereby ye have transgressed; and MAKE YOU A NEW HEART and a new spirit: for why will ye die, O house of Israel? For I have no pleasure in the death of him that dieth, saith the Lord GOD: wherefore turn yourselves, and live ye.

Ezekiel 18:30-32

8. Develop an unblameable heart. An unblameable heart is a heart that is not wrong, evil or injurious in any way.

To the end HE MAY STABLISH YOUR HEARTS UNBLAMEABLE in holiness before God, even our Father, at the coming of our Lord Jesus Christ with all his saints.

1 Thessalonians 3:13

9. Develop a blood-sprinkled heart. A blood sprinkled heart is a heart that is cleansed by the power of God.

Let us draw near with a true heart in full assurance of faith, HAVING OUR HEARTS SPRINKLED from an evil conscience, and our bodies washed with pure water.

Hebrews 10:22

10. Develop a sanctified pure heart. A sanctified pure heart is a heart that has been rendered holy and made free from sin or guilt.

SEEING YE HAVE PURIFIED YOUR SOULS in obeying the truth through the Spirit unto unfeigned love of the brethren, see that ye LOVE ONE ANOTHER WITH A PURE HEART fervently:

1 Peter 1:22

Chapter 42

Be Healed of
Diseased Hearts

Indeed, there are many different kinds of heart problems. It is important to work on your heart so that you are healed of heart disease. Without a normal functioning heart, you cannot accomplish much for the Lord. People with diseased hearts are incapable of doing many things. Every disease in your heart will play itself out in your ministry.

1. **Be healed of a deceived heart. A deceived heart is a deluded heart that has accepted as true or valid what is false.**

   TAKE HEED TO YOURSELVES, THAT YOUR HEART BE NOT DECEIVED, and ye turn aside, and serve other gods, and worship them;

   Deuteronomy 11:16

2. **Be healed of a non-perceiving heart. A non-perceiving heart is a heart that is unable to achieve an understanding of many things. It is not able to recognize, discern or understand the things of God.**

   Yet THE LORD HATH NOT GIVEN YOU AN HEART TO PERCEIVE, and eyes to see, and ears to hear, unto this day.

   Deuteronomy 29:4

3. **Be healed of a fat and greasy heart. A fat and greasy heart is a dull, stupid heart.**

   THEIR HEART IS AS FAT AS GREASE; but I delight in thy law.

   Psalms 119:70

4. **Be healed of a bitter heart. A bitter heart is a heart that is harsh and sarcastic. A bitter heart is also manifested by a showing of great dislike or resentment towards certain people.**

THE HEART KNOWETH HIS OWN BITTERNESS; and a stranger doth not intermeddle with his joy.

Proverbs 14:10

And they shall make themselves utterly bald for thee, and gird them with sackcloth, and THEY SHALL WEEP FOR THEE WITH BITTERNESS OF HEART and bitter wailing.

Ezekiel 27:31

5. **Be healed of a wounded heart. A wounded heart is a heart that is hurt or suffering from an injury. Events that have occurred have broken the hearts of these ones.**

For I am poor and needy, and MY HEART IS WOUNDED WITHIN ME.

Psalms 109:22

6. **Be healed of a weak heart. A weak heart is a heart that is deficient and lacking in strength and vigour. It is a heart that is fragile and liable to break or collapse under pressure or strain.**

HOW WEAK IS THINE HEART, saith the Lord GOD, seeing thou doest all these things, the work of an imperious whorish woman; in that thou buildest thine eminent place in the head of every way, and makest thine high place in every street; and hast not been as an harlot, in that thou scornest hire;

Ezekiel 16:30-31

7. **Be healed of a gross heart. A gross heart is a heart that unrefined and lacking sensitivity or discernment.**

FOR THIS PEOPLE'S HEART IS WAXED GROSS, and their ears are dull of hearing, and their eyes they have closed; lest at any time they should see with their eyes, and hear with their ears, and should understand with their heart, and should be converted, and I should heal them.

Matthew 13:15

8. **Be healed of a lustful heart. A lustful heart is a heart that full of or motivated by lust and greed. It is a lecherous and libidinous heart constantly preoccupied with sexual thoughts and desire.**

So I GAVE THEM UP UNTO THEIR OWN HEARTS' LUST: and they walked in their own counsels.

Psalms 81:12

9. **Be healed of an adulterous heart. An adulterous heart is an unfaithful heart.**

FOR OUT OF THE HEART PROCEED evil thoughts, murders, ADULTERIES, fornications, thefts, false witness, blasphemies:

Matthew 15:19

10. **Be healed of a heart that is blind to God. This heart is unable and unwilling to see, perceive and understand the things of God.**

Having the understanding darkened, being alienated from the life of God through the ignorance that is in them, BECAUSE OF THE BLINDNESS OF THEIR HEART:

Ephesians 4:18

11. **Be healed of a heart that is overwhelmed. An overwhelmed heart is a heart that is overcome completely with emotions and circumstances.**

From the end of the earth will I cry unto thee, WHEN MY HEART IS OVERWHELMED: LEAD ME TO THE ROCK THAT IS HIGHER THAN I.

Psalms 61:2

12. **Be healed of a whorish heart. A whorish heart is a discontented, roaming heart that seeks pleasure from the world.**

And they that escape of you shall remember me among the nations whither they shall be carried captives, because I AM BROKEN WITH THEIR WHORISH HEART, which hath departed from me, and with their eyes, which go a whoring after their idols: and they shall lothe themselves for the evils which they have committed in all their abominations.

Ezekiel 6:9

Chapter 43

Develop an
Encouraging Heart

You can develop an encouraging heart. With an encouraging kind of heart you can accomplish many things for the Lord. The Bible teaches about nine kinds of encouraging hearts. An encouraging heart is a heart that gives hope.

1. **Develop a heart of flesh. A heart of flesh is the soft inside part of a person. It is important that the inside of a person is soft even if the outside looks hard.**

    And I will give them one heart, and I will put a new spirit within you; and I will take the stony heart out of their flesh, and will give them **AN HEART OF FLESH:** that they may walk in my statutes, and keep mine ordinances, and do them: and they shall be my people, and I will be their God.

    Ezekiel 11:19-20

2. **Develop a caring heart. A caring heart is a heart that feels and exhibits concern and empathy for others.**

    But thanks be to God, which put the same **EARNEST CARE INTO THE HEART OF TITUS** for you.

    2 Corinthians 8:16

3. **Develop a singing heart. A singing heart is a heart that is constantly making melody to the Lord. A singing heart is also a cheerful heart.**

    Speaking to yourselves in psalms and hymns and spiritual songs, singing **AND MAKING MELODY IN YOUR HEART** to the Lord;

    Ephesians 5:19

4. **Develop a tender heart. A tender heart is a heart that displays warmth and affection towards others, especially the weaker, poorer and deficient ones.**

BECAUSE THINE HEART WAS TENDER, and thou didst humble thyself before God, when thou heardest his words against this place, and against the inhabitants thereof, and humbledst thyself before me, and didst rend thy clothes, and weep before me; I have even heard thee also, saith the LORD.

2 Chronicles 34:27

5. **Develop a proclaiming heart. A proclaiming heart is one that makes the Gospel known to the public. Someone with a proclaiming heart is loud and emphatic about what he believes.**

MY HEART IS INDITING A GOOD MATTER: I SPEAK OF THE THINGS which I have made touching the king: my tongue is the pen of a ready writer.

Psalms 45:1

6. **Develop a merry heart. A merry heart is quick and energetic. A merry heart shows high-spirited merriment.**

A MERRY HEART DOETH GOOD LIKE A MEDICINE: but a broken spirit drieth the bones.

Proverbs 17:22

7. **Develop an honest and good heart. A person with an honest heart always tells the truth and does not try to deceive people or break the law. An honest heart is a heart that tells the complete truth and gives a sincere opinion even if it is not very pleasant.**

But that on the good ground are they, **WHICH IN AN HONEST AND GOOD HEART, HAVING HEARD THE WORD**, keep it, and bring forth fruit with patience.

Luke 8:15

8. **Develop a circumcised heart. A person with a circumcised heart has had the loose and unwanted aspects of his life cut away.**

But he is a Jew, which is one inwardly; **AND CIRCUMCISION IS THAT OF THE HEART**, in the spirit, and not in the letter; whose praise is not of men, but of God.

Romans 2:29

9. **Develop an enlarged heart. An enlarged heart is a heart that has a greater than normal capacity. A person with an enlarged heart has the capacity to relate with all kinds of people and endure any kind of abuse, inconvenience, embarrassment or bad treatment.**

O ye Corinthians, our mouth is open unto you, **OUR HEART IS ENLARGED**.

2 Corinthians 6:11

Chapter 44

Beware of Developing
a Negative Heart

The Bible also describes different kinds of negative hearts. It is important to work on your heart so that you avoid having a negative heart. Without the right kind of heart you cannot accomplish much for the Lord. A negative heart at the centre of your ministry will release the power of Satan into your ministry. Let us look at fourteen different kinds of negative hearts.

1. **Beware of a presumptuous heart. A presumptuous heart is an overconfident, forward heart that is bold in going beyond the limit of what is appropriate or acceptable. A presumptuous heart arrogantly assumes that privileges must be given to him.**

   Then the king Ahasuerus answered and said unto Esther the queen, WHO IS HE, AND WHERE IS HE, THAT DURST PRESUME IN HIS HEART TO DO SO?

   Esther 7:5

2. **Beware of a despising heart. A despising heart is a heart that is full of scorn. A person with a despising heart looks down on people and has a low opinion of others.**

   And say, How have I hated instruction, AND MY HEART DESPISED REPROOF;

   Proverbs 5:12

3. **Beware of an abominable heart. An abominable heart is a detestable heart. It contains many unpleasant, shocking and disgusting things.**

   When he speaketh fair, believe him not: FOR THERE ARE SEVEN ABOMINATIONS IN HIS HEART.

   Proverbs 26:25

4. **Beware of a despiteful heart. A despiteful heart is a heart that is full of malice and is motivated by spite.**

Thus saith the Lord GOD; because the Philistines have dealt by revenge, AND HAVE TAKEN VENGEANCE WITH A DESPITEFUL HEART, to destroy it for the old hatred;

Ezekiel 25:15

5. **Beware of a beastly heart. A beastly heart is an ill-natured and cantankerous heart. It is a heart that exhibits a lack of human sensibilities.**

Let his heart be changed from man's, and let A BEAST'S HEART BE GIVEN UNTO HIM; and let seven times pass over him.

Daniel 4:16

6. **Beware of an iniquitous heart. An iniquitous heart is characterized by injustice and wickedness. It is a wicked and sinful heart.**

And if he come to see me, he speaketh vanity: HIS HEART GATHERETH INIQUITY TO ITSELF; when he goeth abroad, he telleth it.

Psalms 41:6

7. **Beware of a wicked heart. A wicked heart is a heart that is predisposed to mischief. A wicked heart is bad and deliberately harmful to people.**

Yea, IN HEART YE WORK WICKEDNESS; ye weigh the violence of your hands in the earth.

Psalms 58:2

8. **Beware of a covetous heart. A covetous heart is a heart that has a strong desire to acquire and possess something that belongs to other people.**

Having eyes full of adultery, and that cannot cease from sin; beguiling unstable souls: AN HEART THEY

HAVE EXERCISED WITH COVETOUS PRACTICES;
CURSED CHILDREN:

2 Peter 2:14

9. **Beware of a blasphemous heart. A blasphemous heart is a heart that is grossly irreverent toward what is held to be sacred. It is a heart that is full of profanity or cursing.**

FOR OUT OF THE HEART PROCEED evil thoughts, murders, adulteries, fornications, thefts, false witness, BLASPHEMIES:

Matthew 15:19

10. **Beware of a hypocritical heart. A hypocritical heart is a heart that professes virtues it does not have. A hypocritical heart pretends to have qualities, beliefs and feelings that it does not really have. The hypocritical heart is the heart of a pretender.**

BUT THE HYPOCRITES IN HEART HEAP UP WRATH: they cry not when he bindeth them.

Job 36:13

11. **Beware of a deceitful heart. A deceitful heart is a heart that is false and insincere. A deceitful heart is full of lies. You can never tell when he is speaking the truth and when it is a lie.**

DECEIT IS IN THE HEART OF THEM THAT IMAGINE EVIL: but to the counsellors of peace is joy.

Proverbs 12:20

12. **Beware of an envious, strifeful heart. This heart is painfully desirous of another's advantages or achievements.**

But IF YE HAVE BITTER ENVYING AND STRIFE IN YOUR HEARTS, GLORY NOT, and lie not against the truth.

James 3:14

13. **Beware of an evil heart. An evil heart is a wicked and malicious heart. It is characterized by anger and spite. An evil heart is the cause and source of much destruction and harm.**

And GOD saw that the wickedness of man was great in the earth, and that EVERY IMAGINATION OF THE THOUGHTS OF HIS HEART WAS ONLY EVIL continually.

Genesis 6:5

14. **Beware of a heart that is lifted up. This is a heart that feels good because of something it has become or something it possesses. This is a heart which forgets where it came from. It is the heart which does not remember its humble beginnings.**

Then THINE HEART BE LIFTED UP, and thou forget the LORD thy God, which brought thee forth out of the land of Egypt, from the house of bondage;

Deuteronomy 8:14

And all the people shall know, even Ephraim and THE INHABITANT OF SAMARIA, THAT SAY IN THE PRIDE AND STOUTNESS OF HEART,

Isaiah 9:9

Chapter 45

Develop a
Thoughtful Heart

It is important to work on your heart so that you develop a thoughtful heart. A heart which meditates on the Word and thinks on the right things will be a blessing to the ministry. The thoughts at the centre of your being will definitely affect all that you do.

1. **Develop a broken heart. A broken heart is a heart that is ruined and unsuccessful. It is a heart that has experienced trauma and is disturbed, subdued and oppressed.**

   The LORD is nigh unto them that are of A **BROKEN HEART**; and saveth such as be of a contrite spirit.

   Psalms 34:18

2. **Develop an understanding heart. A person with an understanding heart knows how things work. A few words make a person with an understanding heart know what you mean. A person with an understanding heart shows that he realises how someone feels. An understanding heart is kind and forgiving. A person with an understanding heart is not hostile to someone who has made a mistake.**

   So that thou incline thine ear unto wisdom, and **APPLY THINE HEART TO UNDERSTANDING**;

   Proverbs 2:2

3. **Develop a retaining heart. A retaining heart keeps the words that are spoken to it. A retaining heart keeps possession of and hangs onto every word that is ministered to it. When a person does not have a retaining heart, hours of counselling and preaching are wasted on him.**

He taught me also, and said unto me, **LET THINE HEART RETAIN** my words: keep my commandments, and live.

Proverbs 4:4

Let them not depart from thine eyes; **KEEP THEM IN THE MIDST OF THINE HEART**.

Proverbs 4:21

4. **Develop a heart that is in anguish. A heart that is in anguish is suffering in sorrow, heartache and distress. Usually, a person with an anguished heart is grieving and heartbroken.**

   FOR OUT OF MUCH AFFLICTION AND ANGUISH OF HEART I WROTE unto you with many tears; not that ye should be grieved, but that ye might know the love which I have more abundantly unto you.

   2 Corinthians 2:4

5. **Develop a heavy heart. A person with a heavy heart is sorrowful and downcast. Often, such people appear serious, deep and complex.**

   Give strong drink unto him that is ready to perish, **AND WINE UNTO THOSE THAT BE OF HEAVY HEARTS**.

   Proverbs 31:6

6. **Develop a sorrowful heart. A sorrowful heart is a heart filled with great unhappiness. Usually, a person with a sorrowful heart is miserable, afflicted and appears dejected. It is easy to see a sorrowful heart from the outside.**

   And it came to pass in the month Nisan, in the twentieth year of Artaxerxes the king, that wine was before him: and I took up the wine, and gave it unto the king. Now I had not been beforetime sad in his presence.

184

Wherefore the king said unto me, Why is thy countenance sad, seeing thou art not sick? this is nothing else but **SORROW OF HEART**. Then I was very sore afraid,

And said unto the king, Let the king live for ever: why should not my countenance be sad, when the city, the place of my fathers' sepulchres, lieth waste, and the gates thereof are consumed with fire?

Nehemiah 2:1-3

7. **Develop a pondering heart. A pondering heart is a thoughtful brooding heart. Usually, a person with a pondering heart considers, weighs and studies every subject deeply.**

But Mary kept all these things, and **PONDERED THEM IN HER HEART**.

Luke 2:19

8. **Develop a wise heart. A wise heart is characterized by scholarly knowledge. A wise heart has the power of discerning and judging properly as to what is true or right. A wise heart has information about relevant facts and circumstances. Usually such people are intelligent, sensible and practical.**

Them hath he filled with **WISDOM OF HEART**, to work all manner of work, of the engraver, and of the cunning workman, and of the embroiderer, in blue, and in purple, in scarlet, and in fine linen, and of the weaver, even of them that do any work, and of those that devise cunning work.

Exodus 35:35

Chapter 46

Fight against
Unbending Hearts

There are unbending hearts which never yield, never give in, never give up, never say yes, never say no, never agree, never flow and never submit. It is important to avoid having an unbending heart. Without the right kind of heart you cannot accomplish much for the Lord. Because the heart is the centre of your ministry, it will determine the outcome of everything you do.

1. **Fight against a firm stony heart. A stony heart is a heart that does not show any sympathy or friendliness.**

   HIS HEART IS AS FIRM AS A STONE; yea, as hard as a piece of the nether millstone.

   Job 41:24

2. **Fight against a backslidden heart. A backslidden heart is a heart that has dropped to a lower level or standard. A person with a backslidden heart has failed to serve the Lord as he promised and agreed to. Usually, a person with a backslidden heart has begun to do something undesirable that he had previously stopped.**

   THE BACKSLIDER IN HEART SHALL BE FILLED with his own ways: and a good man shall be satisfied from himself.

   Proverbs 14:14

3. **Fight against a foolish heart. A foolish heart is a heart that is not sensible and shows a lack of judgement.**

   The lips of the wise disperse knowledge: but the **HEART OF THE FOOLISH DOETH NOT SO**.

   Proverbs 15:7

4. **Fight against an erring heart. A person with an erring heart has wandered away from a right course.**

    Forty years long was I grieved with this generation, and said, **IT IS A PEOPLE THAT DO ERR IN THEIR HEART**, and they have not known my ways:

    Psalms 95:10

5. **Fight against a troubled heart. A troubled heart is a worried heart. A troubled heart has many problems and conflicts that swirl within.**

    LET NOT YOUR HEART BE TROUBLED: ye believe in God, believe also in me.

    John 14:1

6. **Fight against a stiff-necked heart. A stiff-necked heart is full of pride and unwilling to do what other people want. Above all, a stiff-necked heart does not want to do what God wants.**

    YE STIFFNECKED AND UNCIRCUMCISED IN HEART AND EARS, ye do always resist the Holy Ghost: as your fathers did, so do ye.

    Acts 7:51

Chapter 47

Develop
Optimistic Hearts

Be positive! Develop optimistic hearts. Expect great things from God. It is important to work on your heart so that you develop an optimistic heart. Without a positive and optimistic outlook you will not accomplish much for the Lord.

1. **Develop a believing heart. A believing heart is a heart that has accepted and taken God's Word to be true. It is a heart that has a firm conviction as to the reality and the goodness of God.**

   That if thou shalt confess with thy mouth the Lord Jesus, AND SHALT BELIEVE IN THINE HEART that God hath raised him from the dead, thou shalt be saved.

   For WITH THE HEART MAN BELIEVETH unto righteousness; and with the mouth confession is made unto salvation.

   Romans 10:9-10

2. **Develop a faithful heart. A faithful heart is a heart that is loyal, constant and reliable. A loyal heart is steady in its allegiance and affection.**

   AND FOUNDEST HIS HEART FAITHFUL BEFORE THEE, and madest a covenant with him to give the land of the Canaanites, the Hittites, the Amorites, and the Perizzites, and the Jebusites, and the Girgashites, to give it, I say, to his seed, and hast performed thy words; for thou art righteous:

   Nehemiah 9:8

3. **Develop a fixed heart. A fixed heart is a heart that is incapable of being changed, moved or undone.**

MY HEART IS FIXED, O God, my heart is fixed: I will sing and give praise.

Psalms 57:7

4. **Develop a purposeful heart. A purposeful heart is a heart that is full of determination.**

BUT DANIEL PURPOSED IN HIS HEART that he would not defile himself with the portion of the king's meat, nor with the wine which he drank: therefore he requested of the prince of the eunuchs that he might not defile himself.

Daniel 1:8

5. **Develop an established heart. An established heart is a heart that is unconditionally settled.**

Be not carried about with divers and strange doctrines. FOR IT IS A GOOD THING THAT THE HEART BE ESTABLISHED WITH GRACE; not with meats, which have not profited them that have been occupied therein.

Hebrews 13:9

Section 4

MINISTRY REALITIES

Chapter 48

How You Can
Enlarge Your Ministry

It is possible for your ministry to be enlarged. It is possible for all that you do to take on a new dimension. God is able to make you preach to more people. God is able to give you larger crowds. God can give you a larger congregation and a larger building. How will this enlargement come about. I want to share eleven steps that will bring enlargement to your life and ministry.

Seven Steps to Enlarging Your Ministry

1. ENLARGE YOUR HEART.

Then thou shalt see, and flow together, and THINE HEART SHALL fear, and BE ENLARGED; because the abundance of the sea shall be converted unto thee, the forces of the Gentiles shall come unto thee.

Isaiah 60:5

O ye Corinthians, our mouth is open unto you, OUR HEART IS ENLARGED.

2 Corinthians 6:11

The size of your work depends on the size of your heart. Some years ago, God touched my heart with a love for the nation Ghana. At certain times, I would sense special warm love for the nation Ghana and its people. God was enlarging my heart so that my ministry would affect the people of Ghana. After that, the Lord enlarged my ministry to touch the whole nation.

At another point in ministry, I sensed a special love in my heart for people who were not Ghanaians. Once again, the Lord was touching my heart again to reach a non-Ghanaian community. Soon I began to see non-Ghanaians drawn to my ministry.

It is so important that God enlarges your heart; otherwise, you will not enter into certain aspects of ministry.

2. ENLARGE YOUR STEPS.

THOU HAST ENLARGED MY STEPS under me; so that my feet did not slip.

2 Samuel 22:37

In order to enlarge your ministry, you must also enlarge your steps. Enlarging your steps speaks of expanding your walk with God. You will have to go deeper if you want to do more. You must pray more, read your Bible more, listen to tapes more, soak in messages more until your ministry is enlarged.

3. ENLARGE YOUR CONFESSION.

And Hannah prayed, and said, My heart rejoiceth in the LORD, mine horn is exalted in the LORD: MY MOUTH IS ENLARGED over mine enemies; because I rejoice in thy salvation.

1 Samuel 2:1

In order to enlarge your ministry, you must enlarge your confession. You must say greater things than you have said in the past. You must change how you speak about your ministry. You must speak of your ministry as something that is enlarged and blessed.

You must say good things about your members, your pastors and your helpers. Your greater confessions will lead to a greater ministry. There was a time when I had to change our church's name because its old name was a restrictive confession. I enlarged my confession and gave my ministry an international name. Through the help of the Holy Spirit, this enlarged confession led to an enlarged ministry.

Your enlarged confession is evidence of your greater vision. Your greater vision will lead to a greater ministry.

Where there is no vision, the people perish: but he that keepeth the law, happy is he.

Proverbs 29:18

4. ENLARGE THE SCOPE OF YOUR MINISTRY.

Not boasting of things without our measure, that is, of other men's labours; but having hope, when your faith is increased, that WE SHALL BE ENLARGED BY YOU ACCORDING TO OUR RULE ABUNDANTLY, TO PREACH THE GOSPEL IN THE REGIONS BEYOND YOU, and not to boast in another man's line of things made ready to our hand.

2 Corinthians 10:15-16

Most people have a specific line of ministry. Perhaps you are a pastor and are not much of a teacher. Perhaps you are a teacher but are not given to the prophetic ministry. In order to enlarge your ministry, you may have to venture into other aspects of ministry, including things you have hitherto despised.

As I have grown in the ministry, I have noticed myself expanding into different spheres of ministry.

I entered into book writing, I entered into missionary work and then I entered into evangelism. All these were new lines of ministry. Each line of ministry brought its own measure of increase eventually. Enlargement comes by branching out into the diverse aspects of ministry.

5. ENLARGE YOUR BORDERS.

For I will cast out the nations before thee, AND ENLARGE THY BORDERS: neither shall any man desire thy land, when thou shalt go up to appear before the LORD thy God thrice in the year.

Exodus 34:24

When the LORD THY GOD SHALL ENLARGE THY BORDER, as he hath promised thee, and thou shalt

say, I will eat flesh, because thy soul longeth to eat flesh;
thou mayest eat flesh, whatsoever thy soul lusteth after.

Deuteronomy 12:20

Enlarging your borders speaks of going beyond your physical and geographical boundaries. Some ministries are limited to local communities, others to cities and others to specific nations. Some ministries are regional or even worldwide. Our church was once called Korle-Bu Christian Centre but I felt it would restrict us to the Korle-Bu community and I sensed that God was giving us a larger ministry.

Through the help of the Holy Spirit, the ministry has grown from a community ministry into an international ministry.

6. *ENLARGE YOUR TERRITORY.*

And Jabez called on the God of Israel saying, "Oh, that YOU WOULD BLESS ME INDEED, AND ENLARGE MY TERRITORY, that Your hand would be with me, and that You would keep me from evil, that I may not cause pain!" So God granted him what he requested.

1 Chronicles 4:10 (NKJV)

It is a blessing to have your territory enlarged. Enlarging your territory speaks of enlarging the sphere in which you have influence. Your ministry may not be physically located in certain places, but God may have given it to you as a territory of influence. For instance, Kenneth Hagin never came to West Africa but countries in this region were greatly under his ministry's influence.

7. *ENLARGE YOUR HABITATION.*

Enlarge the place of thy tent, and let them stretch forth the curtains of thine habitations: spare not, lengthen thy cords, and strengthen thy stakes;

Isaiah 54:2

Enlarging your habitation speaks of expanding the ground on which your tent stands. The Scripture above reveals a commandment to lengthen the cords and strengthen the stakes for an enlarged tent. Basically, enlarging your habitation speaks of enlarging your preparations for ministry.

Preparation has a great impact on the outcome of any ministry. Jesus Christ did not go into the ministry without the extensive preparation of forerunners like John the Baptist. He also sent out seventy people to go ahead and prepare the way before Him. Jesus Christ believed greatly in "preparation".

When you increase the preparation that you make for preaching and ministering, the effect will show up in your ministry. There is no labour without profit!

The crusade ministry gave me a first-hand experience with the power of expanded preparatory efforts. Our crusade attendance jumped dramatically when the preparation for the crusade was intensified and lengthened. When I learnt that Billy Graham would spend up to two years preparing for a single crusade, I realised the effect that preparation had on any ministry.

Chapter 49

A Shepherd is a Light

And God made two great lights; THE GREATER LIGHT to rule the day, and THE LESSER LIGHT to rule the night: he made the stars also.

Genesis 1:16

God made two types of lights: greater lights and lesser lights. These lights were to rule the day and the night. In the ministry, there are also greater lights and lesser lights. God has made greater lights and lesser lights to shine the Gospel into this world. Some ministries are "greater" lights and others are "lesser" lights.

The ministry is described as a light. Jesus often referred to Himself as a light. He also reminded His disciples to be lights that shine forth. The disciples of Jesus were going to be lights in the world.

1. **JESUS CHRIST IS THE GREATEST LIGHT TO EVER SHINE IN THIS WORLD. Several times in the Gospels, He described Himself as the light that had come into the world.**

And leaving Nazareth, he came and dwelt in Capernaum, which is upon the sea coast, in the borders of Zabulon and Nephthalim:

That it might be fulfilled which was spoken by Esaias the prophet, saying,

The land of Zabulon, and the land of Nephthalim, by the way of the sea, beyond Jordan, Galilee of the Gentiles;

The people which sat in darkness saw GREAT LIGHT; and to them which sat in the region and shadow of death light is sprung up.

Matthew 4:13-16

In him was life; AND THE LIFE WAS THE LIGHT OF MEN. And the light shineth in darkness; and the darkness comprehended it not.

John 1:4-5

The same came for a witness, to bear witness of the Light, that all men through him might believe. He was not that Light, but was sent to bear witness of that Light. THAT WAS THE TRUE LIGHT, which lighteth every man that cometh into the world.

John 1:7-9

And this is the condemnation, THAT LIGHT IS COME INTO THE WORLD, and men loved darkness rather than light, because their deeds were evil.

John 3:19

Then spake Jesus again unto them, saying, I AM THE LIGHT OF THE WORLD: he that followeth me shall not walk in darkness, but shall have the light of life.

John 8:12

As long as I am in the world, I AM THE LIGHT OF THE WORLD.

John 9:5

Then Jesus said unto them, YET A LITTLE WHILE IS THE LIGHT WITH YOU. Walk while ye have the light, lest darkness come upon you: for he that walketh in darkness knoweth not whither he goeth.

While ye have light, believe in the light, that ye may be the children of light. These things spake Jesus, and departed, and did hide himself from them.

John 12:35-36

Jesus cried and said, He that believeth on me, believeth not on me, but on him that sent me. And he that seeth me seeth him that sent me. I AM COME A LIGHT into the world, that whosoever believeth on me should not abide in darkness.

John 12:44-46

2. JOHN THE BAPTIST WAS ALSO DESCRIBED AS A LIGHT.

He was not that Light, but was sent to bear witness of that Light.

John 1:8

He was a burning and a shining light: and ye were willing for a season to rejoice in his light.

John 5:35

3. EVERY MINISTER IS A BURNING FLAME THAT BRINGS LIGHT INTO THE WORLD. Your ministry is a light that is shining forth into the darkness of the world.

Let your light so shine before men, that they may see your good works, and glorify your Father which is in heaven.

Matthew 5:16

And of the angels he saith, Who maketh his angels spirits, and his ministers a flame of fire.

Hebrews 1:7

Chapter 50

Why Some People
Are Greater Lights

Four Reasons Why Some People
Are Greater Lights

1. **The sovereign decision of God makes some people greater lights.**

For thou art an holy people unto the Lord thy God: the Lord thy God hath chosen thee to be a special people unto himself, above all people that are upon the face of the earth.

Deuteronomy 7:6

Only the Lord had a delight in thy fathers to love them, and he chose their seed after them, even you above all people, as it is this day.

Deuteronomy 10:15

For thou art an holy people unto the Lord thy God, and the Lord hath chosen thee to be a peculiar people unto himself, above all the nations that are upon the earth.

Deuteronomy 14:2

2. **The favour of God makes some people greater lights.**

Only the Lord had a delight in thy fathers to love them, and he chose their seed after them, even you above all people, as it is this day.

Deuteronomy 10:15

Now when the turn of Esther, the daughter of Abihail the uncle of Mordecai, who had taken her for his daughter, was come to go in unto the king, she required nothing but what

Hegai the king's chamberlain, the keeper of the women, appointed. And Esther obtained favour in the sight of all them that looked upon her. So Esther was taken unto king Ahasuerus into his house royal in the tenth month, which is the month Tebeth, in the seventh year of his reign. And the king loved Esther above all the women, and she obtained grace and favour in his sight more than all the virgins; so that he set the royal crown upon her head, and made her queen instead of Vashti.

Esther 2:15-17

3. Being given more than one gift or talent makes some people greater lights.

And unto one he gave five talents, to another two, and to another one; to every man according to his several ability; and straightway took his journey.

Matthew 25:15

And Israel said unto Joseph, Behold, I die: but God shall be with you, and bring you again unto the land of your fathers. Moreover I have given to thee one portion above thy brethren, which I took out of the hand of the Amorite with my sword and with my bow.

Genesis 48:21-22

4. The blessings of a father make some people greater lights.

Shem, Ham and Japheth turned out differently in this world because of the blessings their father spoke over their lives. Indeed, the blessing of a father determines the outcome of your ministry. That is what determines whether you will be a greater light or a lesser light. You must strive to obtain great blessings from your spiritual father. You must avoid any kind of curse from your father. The greater the blessings of your father, the greater the light that will shine forth from your life.

Also, you will notice that Joseph had blessings from his father that were even greater than the blessings of his ancestors.

These superior blessings caused him to be a greater light: "The blessings of your father have surpassed the blessings of my ancestors up to the utmost bound of the everlasting hills; May they be on the head of Joseph, and on the crown of the head of the one distinguished among his brothers" (Genesis 49:26, NASB).

And he said, Cursed be Canaan; a servant of servants shall he be unto his brethren. And he said, Blessed be the LORD God of Shem; and Canaan shall be his servant.

God shall enlarge Japheth, and he shall dwell in the tents of Shem; and Canaan shall be his servant.

Genesis 9:25-27

Chapter 51

How You Can Become a Greater Light

1. Obedience will make you a greater light.

Now therefore, if ye will obey my voice indeed, and keep my covenant, then ye shall be a peculiar treasure unto me above all people: for all the earth is mine:

Exodus 19:5

Wherefore it shall come to pass, if ye hearken to these judgments, and keep, and do them, that the Lord thy God shall keep unto thee the covenant and the mercy which he sware unto thy fathers:

And he will love thee, and bless thee, and multiply thee: he will also bless the fruit of thy womb, and the fruit of thy land, thy corn, and thy wine, and thine oil, the increase of thy kine, and the flocks of thy sheep, in the land which he sware unto thy fathers to give thee.

Thou shalt be blessed above all people: there shall not be male or female barren among you, or among your cattle.

And the Lord will take away from thee all sickness, and will put none of the evil diseases of Egypt, which thou knowest, upon thee; but will lay them upon all them that hate thee.

Deuteronomy 7:12-15

2. Humility will make you a greater light.

And whosoever shall exalt himself shall be abased; and he that shall humble himself shall be exalted.

Matthew 23:12

3. Excellence will make you a greater light. Excellence in all you do will lead to promotion. Putting away the shabby, untidy, unkempt and messy things will lead to promotion.

Then this Daniel was preferred above the presidents and princes, because an excellent spirit was in him; and the king thought to set him over the whole realm.

Daniel 6:3

4. **Righteousness will make you a greater light.** Hating iniquity will make you a greater light.

Thou hast loved righteousness, and hated iniquity; therefore God, even thy God, hath anointed thee with the oil of gladness above thy fellows.

Hebrews 1:9

5. **Rejoicing in salvation will make you a greater light.** Focusing on salvation, emphasizing salvation, understanding salvation and preaching about salvation will make you a greater light.

Today, many people do not focus on salvation because they consider it too basic. Salvation is the greatest gift we have ever received from the Lord. Understanding our salvation should be the greatest focus of our Bible studies. Understanding salvation will make us both grateful and fruitful.

And Hannah prayed, and said, My heart rejoiceth in the Lord, mine horn is exalted in the Lord: my mouth is enlarged over mine enemies; because I rejoice in thy salvation.

1 Samuel 2:1

6. **Looking to God for promotion will make you a greater light.** To look to the east, the west and the south to become a greater light is to look in the wrong direction. Do not look to man. Promotion only comes from the Lord.

For promotion *cometh* neither from the east, nor from the west, nor from the south.

Psalm 75:6

Chapter 52

The Spiritual Joints
of Ministry

**From whom the whole body fitly joined together
and compacted by that which every joint supplieth,
according to the effectual working in the measure
of every part, maketh increase of the body unto the
edifying of itself in love.**

Ephesians 4:16

It is time to be mature and to recognize the need for other parts of the body. The arm needs the trunk of the body because the trunk contains the heart. The trunk of the body needs the arm to buy food because the stomach cannot pick up food from the table. This analogy is easy enough for a simpleton to understand. Yet we constantly violate these principles in our spiritual work.

One of the greatest mysteries of ministry is the mystery of the spiritual joints in the Body of Christ. Through joints you are connected to other parts of the Body of Christ. Through joints, you are connected to people who are important for your spiritual development. Through joints, you will be supplied with what you need for effective ministry.

Often, you are connected to something that is very different from yourself. Think about how much bigger the trunk of the body is compared to an arm and a leg. And yet, the huge trunk needs to be connected to the slim arm for happiness and fruitfulness.

Maintaining supple healthy joints are the key to receiving the anointing, a covering and spiritual guidance. One of the greatest examples of spiritual joints was the spiritual joint between Elijah and Elisha. This joint was the connection through which the double portion of the anointing flowed to Elisha's life. Elisha experienced a double portion of the grace of God because he was intensely connected to Elijah. He did not allow anything to break that all-important joint.

Ten Revelations about the Joint between Elijah and Elisha

1. Elisha was joined tightly to Elijah. He could not be separated from Elijah by Elijah himself. Elijah's own advice went against Elisha's love and dedication to Elijah. Elisha saw through the instruction and knew that he was being separated from what he needed.

   And Elijah said unto Elisha, Tarry here, I pray thee; for the LORD hath sent me to Bethel. And Elisha said unto him, As the LORD liveth, and as thy soul liveth, I will not leave thee. So they went down to Bethel.

   2 Kings 2:2

2. Elisha was joined tightly to Elijah. He could not be separated from his mentor *as long as the Lord was alive.*

   And Elijah said unto Elisha, Tarry here, I pray thee; for the LORD hath sent me to Bethel. And Elisha said unto him, AS THE LORD LIVETH, and as thy soul liveth, I will not leave thee. So they went down to Bethel.

   2 Kings 2:2

3. Elisha was joined tightly to Elijah. He could not be separated from Elijah *as long as Elijah was alive.*

   And Elijah said unto Elisha, Tarry here, I pray thee; for the LORD hath sent me to Bethel. And Elisha said unto him, As the LORD liveth, AND AS THY SOUL LIVETH, I will not leave thee. So they went down to Bethel.

   2 Kings 2:2

4. Elisha was joined tightly to Elijah. He could not be separated from Elijah by fifty prophets. Many people's lives are destroyed when they listen to false prophets.

    And the sons of the prophets that were at Bethel came forth to Elisha, and said unto him, Knowest thou that the LORD will take away thy master from thy head to day? And he said, Yea, I know it; hold ye your peace.
    2 Kings 2:3

5. Elisha was joined tightly to Elijah. He could not be separated from Elijah by the events in Gilgal.

    And it came to pass, when the LORD would take up Elijah into heaven by a whirlwind, that Elijah went with Elisha from Gilgal. And Elijah said unto Elisha, Tarry here, I pray thee; for the LORD hath sent me to Bethel. And Elisha said unto him, As the LORD liveth, and as thy soul liveth, I will not leave thee. So they went down to Bethel.
    2 Kings 2:1-2

6. Elisha was joined tightly to Elijah. He could not be separated from Elijah by the circumstances of Bethel.

    And the sons of the prophets that were at Bethel came forth to Elisha, and said unto him, Knowest thou that the LORD will take away thy master from thy head to day? And he said, Yea, I know it; hold ye your peace.
    2 Kings 2:3

7. Elisha was joined tightly to Elijah. He could not be separated from Elijah by the pressures and experiences of Jericho.

    And Elijah said unto him, Elisha, tarry here, I pray thee; for the LORD hath sent me to Jericho. And he said, As the LORD liveth, and as thy soul liveth, I will not leave thee. So they came to Jericho.
    2 Kings 2:4

8. Elisha was joined tightly to Elijah. He could not be separated from Elijah by the pressures of Jordan.

    And Elijah said unto him, Tarry, I pray thee, here; for the LORD hath sent me to Jordan. And he said, As the LORD liveth, and as thy soul liveth, I will not leave thee. And they two went on.

    2 Kings 2:6

9. Elisha was joined tightly to Elijah. His eyes were glued to Elijah up to the very end. Elisha was told that keeping his eyes on Elijah to the very end would be the secret to his receiving the anointing.

    When they had crossed over, Elijah said to Elisha, "Ask what I shall do for you before I am taken from you." And Elisha said, "Please, let a double portion of your spirit be upon me." He said, "You have asked a hard thing. Nevertheless, if you see me when I am taken from you, it shall be so for you; but if not, it shall not be so."

    2 Kings 2:9-10 (NASB)

10. Elisha was joined tightly to Elijah. He could only be separated from his father by something divine. Many ministers are separated from their mentors by carnality, quarrels and envy. Through conflict, people are separated from the very people they need. You must get to the place where only a divine act can separate you from the body that God has joined you to.

    As they were going along and talking, behold, there appeared a chariot of fire and horses of fire which separated the two of them. And Elijah went up by a whirlwind to heaven.

    2 Kings 2:11 (NASB)

Chapter 53

The Stumbling Blocks of Ministry

But he turned and said to Peter, "Get behind Me, satan! You are a stumbling block to Me; for you are not setting your mind on God's interests, but man's."
Matthew 16:23 (NASB)

In this passage, Jesus clearly defined what could become a stumbling block to His ministry. On the surface, you would think that Satan was the stumbling block. However, the stumbling block was something more subtle than that. It was the *interests of men* that were the stumbling blocks to Jesus' ministry.

A stumbling block is a problem which stops you from achieving something. A stumbling block is therefore an obstacle, a difficulty, a problem, a barrier, a hurdle, an impediment or a hindrance to your calling.

Jesus Christ revealed that stumbling blocks are the interests of men! When someone has an interest in something, he focuses on that thing because there are benefits to gain from it. The interests of men yield many benefits to men but the problem is that the interests of men are different from the interests of God!

Not only are the interests of men different from the interests of God, but they hinder ministry and are contradictory to your calling This is why when people pursue these interests they actually destroy their ministries. Over the years, I have watched people pursue the interests of men and end up on the rubbish heap of ministry.

When you do not pursue the "interests of men" it looks as though you do not love yourself! This is because pursuing the interests of men actually improves your life on this earth. I want to emphasize that the interests of men are not satanic or occultic activities. The mystery of these stumbling blocks is that they are often the basic needs of the common man. The interests of men are things like food, clothing, marriage, children, money, houses, cars, security and stability.

Twelve Interests of Men Which Are Stumbling Blocks to Your Calling

1. Food and clothing are not evil things. However, your pursuit of food and clothing can become a stumbling block to your calling.

2. Marriage is not evil but your pursuit of marriage can be a stumbling block to your calling.

3. Having children and bringing them up are not evil but your pursuit of these can become a stumbling block to your ministry.

4. Money is not an evil thing, but your pursuit of money is a stumbling block to your calling.

5. Having a house is not an evil thing but your pursuit of houses will be a stumbling block to your calling.

6. Cars are not evil things but your pursuit of cars can be a stumbling block to your calling.

7. Living in a particular location is not an evil thing but your relentless desire to live in certain places is a stumbling block to your calling.

8. Being important is not evil but your pursuit of self-importance will be a stumbling block to your calling.

9. Safety is not an evil thing but your relentless pursuit of safety and security is a stumbling block to your calling.

10. An improved earthly existence is not evil but your desire for the upper-class life will be a stumbling block to your calling.

11. Establishment is not an evil thing but your relentless pursuit of an established life will be a stumbling block to your calling.

12. Education is not an evil thing but your relentless lifelong pursuit for education is a stumbling block to your calling.

Chapter 54

Overcoming Delays
in the Evil Day

Put on the whole armour of God, that ye may be able to stand against the wiles of the devil.

For we wrestle not against flesh and blood, but against principalities, against powers, against the rulers of the darkness of this world, against spiritual wickedness in high places.

Wherefore take unto you the whole armour of God, THAT YE MAY BE ABLE TO WITHSTAND IN THE EVIL DAY, and having done all, to stand.

Ephesians 6:11-13

What makes a day an evil day? Delays can turn a day into an evil day! There are several other things that can turn a good day into an evil day. Temptations, tests and trials can cause you to enter into what is called an "evil day". Tests and trials often come about when there is some sort of delay.

All through the Scriptures you see how things changed when there was a delay. Many good people become evil during the period of delay. Notice how the evil servant changed into a drunkard when the lord delayed his coming. "But and if that evil servant shall say in his heart, My lord delayeth his coming; and shall begin to smite his fellow servants, and to eat and drink with the drunken" (Matthew 24:48-49).

Also, during periods of delay, you will see various kinds of human weaknesses in manifestation. "Now while the bridegroom was delaying, they all got drowsy and began to sleep" (Matthew 25:5 (NASB).

A combination of human weakness, temptation and demonic activity combine to create an evil day for you. However, the evil day can turn into a day of victory for you. Depending on the level of understanding you have, you will see the hand of God at work. He will bring you to a perfect end.

In order to overcome the delays that abound in ministry, it is important to do three things.

1. **Actually expect delays in your life and ministry**.

2. **Understand why and how delays come about**. Over and over, Jesus told His disciples how people would fall away during apparent delays in the fulfilment of the promises of God.

3. **Prepare for delays by making extra preparation for possible delays**. Do what the ten virgins did. Take extra oil and make extra preparations to be able to last in the longest possible delay that may occur in your life and ministry.

   ... but the prudent took oil in flasks along wit their lamps

   Matthew 25:4 (NASB)

Twenty Delays You Must Expect

1. You must expect a delay in the coming of the Lord.

Be patient therefore, brethren, unto the coming of the Lord. Behold, the husbandman waiteth for the precious fruit of the earth, and hath long patience for it, until he receive the early and latter rain.

James 5:7

2. You must expect possible delays in the fulfilment of some of God's promises to you.

The Lord is not slack concerning his promise, as some men count slackness; but is longsuffering to us-ward, not willing that any should perish, but that all should come to repentance.

2 Peter 3:9

3. You must expect possible delays in getting married.

And Jacob loved Rachel; and said, I will serve thee seven years for Rachel thy younger daughter. And Laban said, It is better that I give her to thee, than that I should give her to another man: abide with me. And Jacob served seven years for Rachel; and they seemed unto him but a few days, for the love he had to her.

Genesis 29:18-20

Fulfil her week, and we will give thee this also for the service which thou shalt serve with me yet seven other years.

And Jacob did so, and fulfilled her week: and he gave him Rachel his daughter to wife also.

Genesis 29:27-28

4. You must expect possible delays in childbirth.

And when the time was that Elkanah offered, he gave to Peninnah his wife, and to all her sons and her daughters, portions:

But unto Hannah he gave a worthy portion; for he loved Hannah: but the LORD had shut up her womb.

And her adversary also provoked her sore, for to make her fret, because the Lord had shut up her womb.

And as he did so year by year, when she went up to the house of the Lord, so she provoked her; therefore she wept, and did not eat.

1 Samuel 1:4-7

And, behold, thy cousin Elisabeth, she hath also conceived a son in her old age: and this is the sixth month with her, who was called barren. For with God nothing shall be impossible.

Luke 1:36-37

5. You must expect possible delays in promotion.

How long wilt thou forget me, O LORD? for ever? how long wilt thou hide thy face from me? How long shall I take counsel in my soul, having sorrow in my heart daily? how long shall mine enemy be exalted over me?

Psalm 13:1-2

6. You must expect a delay in the coming of the anointing and the gift of God.

We see not our signs: there is no more any prophet: neither is there among us any that knoweth how long.

O God, how long shall the adversary reproach? shall the enemy blaspheme thy name for ever?

Psalm 74:9-10

7. You must expect delays in people taking decisions.

And Elijah came unto all the people, and said, How long halt ye between two opinions? if the LORD be God, follow him: but if Baal, then follow him. And the people answered him not a word.

1 Kings 18:21

8. You must expect possible delays in God blessing you with a large ministry.

Turn us again, O God, and cause thy face to shine; and we shall be saved.

O LORD God of hosts, how long wilt thou be angry against the prayer of thy people?

Thou feedest them with the bread of tears; and givest them tears to drink in great measure.

Thou makest us a strife unto our neighbours: and our enemies laugh among themselves.

Turn us again, O God of hosts, and cause thy face to shine; and we shall be saved.

Psalm 80:3-7

9. You must expect delays in becoming rich.

Righteous art thou, O LORD, when I plead with thee: yet let me talk with thee of thy judgments: Wherefore doth the way of the wicked prosper? wherefore are all they happy that deal very treacherously?

Thou hast planted them, yea, they have taken root: they grow, yea, they bring forth fruit: thou art near in their mouth, and far from their reins.

But thou, O LORD, knowest me: thou hast seen me, and tried mine heart toward thee: pull them out like sheep for the slaughter, and prepare them for the day of slaughter.

How long shall the land mourn, and the herbs of every field wither, for the wickedness of them that dwell therein? the beasts are consumed, and the birds; because they said, He shall not see our last end.

Jeremiah 12:1-4

10. You must expect delays in the realization of your dreams.

And there remained among the children of Israel seven tribes, which had not yet received their inheritance.

And Joshua said unto the children of Israel, How long are ye slack to go to possess the land, which the LORD God of your fathers hath given you?

Joshua 18:2-3

11. You must expect possible delays in church members learning what you are teaching them.

And Moses said, Eat that to day; for to day is a sabbath unto the LORD: to day ye shall not find it in the field.

Six days ye shall gather it; but on the seventh day, which is the sabbath, in it there shall be none.

And it came to pass, that there went out some of the people on the seventh day for to gather, and they found none.

And the LORD said unto Moses, How long refuse ye to keep my commandments and my laws?

Exodus 16:25-28

12. You must expect delays in obtaining victory over opposition.

And Moses and Aaron came in unto Pharaoh, and said unto him, Thus saith the LORD God of the Hebrews, How long wilt thou refuse to humble thyself before me? let my people go, that they may serve me.

Exodus 10:3

13. You must expect delays in people believing in your calling.

And the LORD said unto Moses, How long will this people provoke me? and how long will it be ere they believe me, for all the signs which I have shewed among them?

Numbers 14:11

14. You must expect delays in overcoming difficult situations.

Then Job answered and said,

How long will ye vex my soul, and break me in pieces with words?

These ten times have ye reproached me: ye are not ashamed that ye make yourselves strange to me.

And be it indeed that I have erred, mine error remaineth with myself.

If indeed ye will magnify yourselves against me, and plead against me my reproach:

Know now that God hath overthrown me, and hath compassed me with his net.

Job 19:1-6

15. You must expect delays in church members changing their lifestyle.

O ye sons of men, how long will ye turn my glory into shame? how long will ye love vanity, and seek after leasing? Selah.

But know that the LORD hath set apart him that is godly for himself: the LORD will hear when I call unto him.

Psalm 4:2-3

16. You must expect delays in healing and miracles.

Have mercy upon me, O LORD; for I am weak: O LORD, heal me; for my bones are vexed. My soul is also sore vexed: but thou, O LORD, how long?

Psalm 6:2-3

17. You must expect delays in the wicked being brought to judgement.

LORD, how long shall the wicked, how long shall the wicked triumph?

How long shall they utter and speak hard things? and all the workers of iniquity boast themselves?

They break in pieces thy people, O LORD, and afflict thine heritage.

They slay the widow and the stranger, and murder the fatherless.

Yet they say, The LORD shall not see, neither shall the God of Jacob regard it.

Psalm 94:3-7

18. You must expect delays in fools becoming wise.

Wisdom crieth without; she uttereth her voice in the streets:

She crieth in the chief place of concourse, in the openings of the gates: in the city she uttereth her words, saying,

How long, ye simple ones, will ye love simplicity? and the scorners delight in their scorning, and fools hate knowledge?

Turn you at my reproof: behold, I will pour out my spirit unto you, I will make known my words unto you.

Proverbs 1:20-23

19. You must expect delays in lazy people becoming hard-working.

How long wilt thou sleep, O sluggard? when wilt thou arise out of thy sleep?

Yet a little sleep, a little slumber, a little folding of the hands to sleep:

So shall thy poverty come as one that travelleth, and thy want as an armed man.

Proverbs 6:9-11

20. You must expect possible delays in the judgement of thieves.

You will realise that most thieves are not caught. They seem to get away with their stealing. But the Scripture cannot be broken, "...whatever a man sows, this he will also reap" (Galatians 6:7, NASB).

Shall not all these take up a parable against him, and a taunting proverb against him, and say, Woe to him that increaseth that which is not his! how long? and to him that ladeth himself with thick clay!

Habbakuk 2:6

Chapter 55

Fifteen Evils That Arise
When There Is a Delay

1. **When there are delays, many people have bad thoughts. Bad thoughts flow freely through the mind of someone who senses a delay of God's blessings.**

   Blessed is that servant, whom his lord when he cometh shall find so doing.

   Verily I say unto you, That he shall make him ruler over all his goods.

   But and if THAT EVIL SERVANT SHALL SAY IN HIS HEART, My lord delayeth his coming;

   And shall begin to smite his fellowservants, and to eat and drink with the drunken;

   The lord of that servant shall come in a day when he looketh not for him, and in an hour that he is not aware of, and shall cut him asunder, and appoint him his portion with the hypocrites: there shall be weeping and gnashing of teeth.

   Matthew 24:46-51

2. **When there are delays, many people have bad ideas. Many different bad ideas occur to people who feel that God's blessing is delayed.**

   AND WHEN THE PEOPLE SAW THAT MOSES DELAYED TO COME DOWN OUT OF THE MOUNT, THE PEOPLE GATHERED THEMSELVES TOGETHER UNTO AARON, AND SAID UNTO HIM, UP, MAKE US GODS, which shall go before us; for as for this Moses, the man that brought us up out of the land of Egypt, we wot not what is become of him.

And Aaron said unto them, Break off the golden earrings, which are in the ears of your wives, of your sons, and of your daughters, and bring them unto me.

And all the people brake off the golden earrings which were in their ears, and brought them unto Aaron.

And he received them at their hand, and fashioned it with a graving tool, after he had made it a molten calf: and they said, These be thy gods, O Israel, which brought thee up out of the land of Egypt. And when Aaron saw it, he built an altar before it; and Aaron made proclamation, and said, To morrow is a feast to the LORD.

Exodus 32:1-5

3. When there are delays, people try to use the arm of flesh to accomplish what only God can do.

And Sarai said unto Abram, Behold now, the LORD hath restrained me from bearing: I pray thee, GO IN UNTO MY MAID; IT MAY BE THAT I MAY OBTAIN CHILDREN BY HER. AND ABRAM HEARKENED TO THE VOICE OF SARAI. And Sarai Abram's wife took Hagar her maid the Egyptian, after Abram had dwelt ten years in the land of Canaan, and gave her to her husband Abram to be his wife. And he went in unto Hagar, and she conceived: and when she saw that she had conceived, her mistress was despised in her eyes.

Genesis 16:2-4

4. When there are delays, many people abandon their original calling.

And the Lord said, Who then is that faithful and wise steward, whom his lord shall make ruler over his household, to give them their portion of meat in due season?

BLESSED IS THAT SERVANT, WHOM HIS LORD WHEN HE COMETH SHALL FIND SO DOING.

Of a truth I say unto you, that he will make him ruler over all that he hath.

But and if that servant say in his heart, My lord delayeth his coming; and shall begin to beat the menservants and maidens, and to eat and drink, and to be drunken;

Luke 12:42-45

5. **When there are delays, people blame the leaders for their problems.**

AND THEY SAID UNTO MOSES, BECAUSE THERE WERE NO GRAVES IN EGYPT, hast thou taken us away to die in the wilderness? wherefore hast thou dealt thus with us, to carry us forth out of Egypt? Is not this the word that we did tell thee in Egypt, saying, Let us alone, that we may serve the Egyptians? For it had been better for us to serve the Egyptians, than that we should die in the wilderness.

Exodus 14:11-12

6. **When there are delays, people become bitter. They resent God and they resent their church. People leave their churches and go elsewhere. Others join prophetic movements, seeking help and answers to unanswered prayer.**

Then said Elkanah her husband to her, Hannah, why weepest thou? and why eatest thou not? and why is thy heart grieved? AM NOT I BETTER TO THEE THAN TEN SONS?

So Hannah rose up after they had eaten in Shiloh, and after they had drunk. Now Eli the priest sat upon a seat by a post of the temple of the LORD.

And SHE WAS IN BITTERNESS OF SOUL, and prayed unto the LORD, and wept sore.

And she vowed a vow, and said, O Lord of hosts, if thou wilt indeed look on the affliction of thine handmaid, and remember me, and not forget thine handmaid, but wilt give unto thine handmaid a man child, then I will give him unto the LORD all the days of his life, and there shall no rasor come upon his head.

1 Samuel 1:8-11

7. When there are delays, many people begin to believe things they should not believe.

And except those days should be shortened, there should no flesh be saved: but for the elect's sake those days shall be shortened.

Then if any man shall say unto you, Lo, here is Christ, or there; believe it not.

For there shall arise false Christs, and false prophets, and shall shew great signs and wonders; insomuch that, if it were possible, they shall deceive the very elect.

Matthew 24:22-24

8. When there are delays, many people are caught unprepared.

Now while bridegroom was delaying, they all got drowsy and began to sleep. But at midnight there was a shout, "Behold, the bridegroom! Come out to meet him." Then all those virgins rose and trimmed their lamps. The foolish said to the prudent, "Give us some of your oil, for our lamps are going out."

Matthew 25: 5-8 (NASB)

9. When there are delays, many people backslide and their lights go out.

Then shall the kingdom of heaven be likened unto ten virgins, which took their lamps, and went forth to meet the bridegroom. And five of them were wise, and five were foolish. They that were foolish took their lamps, and took no oil with them: but the wise took oil in their vessels with their lamps. While the bridegroom tarried, they all slumbered and slept.

And at midnight there was a cry made, Behold, the bridegroom cometh; go ye out to meet him. Then all those virgins arose, and trimmed their lamps.

And the foolish said unto the wise, Give us of your oil; for OUR LAMPS ARE GONE OUT.

But the wise answered, saying, Not so; lest there be not enough for us and you: but go ye rather to them that sell, and buy for yourselves.

Matthew 25:1-9

10. When there are delays, people become wicked.

But and if that EVIL SERVANT shall say in his heart, My lord delayeth his coming; and shall begin to smite his fellowservants, and to eat and drink with the drunken;

Matthew 24:48-49

11. When there are delays, many people lose their position.

While the bridegroom tarried, they all slumbered and slept.

Afterward came also the other virgins, saying, Lord, Lord, open to us.

But he answered and said, Verily I say unto you, I KNOW YOU NOT.

Mathew 25:5, 11-12

12. When there are delays, many people become hypocrites.

But and if that evil servant shall say in his heart, My lord delayeth his coming; And shall begin to smite his fellowservants, and to eat and drink with the drunken;

The lord of that servant shall come in a day when he looketh not for him, and in an hour that he is not aware of, and shall cut him asunder, and appoint him HIS PORTION WITH THE HYPOCRITES: there shall be weeping and gnashing of teeth.

Matthew 24:48-51

13. When there are delays, ministers start to fight each other.

But and if that evil servant shall say in his heart, My lord delayeth his coming; and SHALL BEGIN TO SMITE HIS FELLOWSERVANTS, and to eat and drink with the drunken;

Matthew 24:48-49

14. When there are delays, many people deviate from their calling.

BLESSED IS THAT SERVANT, WHOM HIS LORD WHEN HE COMETH SHALL FIND SO DOING.

Verily I say unto you, That he shall make him ruler over all his goods. But and if that evil servant shall say in his heart, My lord delayeth his coming; and shall begin to smite his fellowservants, and to eat and drink with the drunken;

The lord of that servant shall come in a day when he looketh not for him, and in an hour that he is not aware of, and shall cut him asunder, and appoint him his portion with the hypocrites: there shall be weeping and gnashing of teeth.

Matthew 24:46-51

15. When there are delays, people ignore the Word of God and carry on with their lives as if there is no God.

But as the days of Noe were, so shall also the coming of the Son of man be.

For as in the days that were before the flood THEY WERE EATING AND DRINKING, MARRYING AND GIVING IN MARRIAGE, UNTIL THE DAY THAT NOE ENTERED INTO THE ARK, And knew not until the flood came, and took them all away; so shall also the coming of the Son of man be.

Then shall two be in the field; the one shall be taken, and the other left. Two women shall be grinding at the mill; the one shall be taken, and the other left.

Matthew 24:37-41

Chapter 56

Eight Reasons
Why Delays Occur

1. *God has a determined time for everything.* God will not sacrifice His divinity and sovereignty to impress you or me. He will do exactly what He wants. And He will do it when He wants to.

   To every thing there is a season, and a time to every purpose under the heaven:
   Ecclesiastes 3:1

   Is there not an appointed time to man upon earth? are not his days also like the days of an hireling?
   Job 7:1

2. *God wants us to experience certain tests.* He allows us to be tested by delaying certain things. He searches us to know what is in our hearts. He wants to see our response to delays. A delay will bring out what is in us.

   And thou shalt remember all the way which the LORD thy God led thee these forty years in the wilderness, to humble thee, and to prove thee, to know what was in thine heart, whether thou wouldest keep his commandments, or no.
   Deuteronomy 8:2

3. *Delays occur so that you can get yourself ready for the blessings that are to come.* It is very important to be prepared for the blessings of God. The woman in the story below had to prepare to receive the oil.

   Now there cried a certain woman of the wives of the sons of the prophets unto Elisha, saying, Thy servant my husband is dead; and thou knowest that thy servant did fear the LORD: and the creditor is come to take unto him my two sons to be bondmen. And Elisha said unto

225

her, What shall I do for thee? tell me, what hast thou in the house? And she said, Thine handmaid hath not any thing in the house, save a pot of oil. Then he said, Go, borrow thee vessels abroad of all thy neighbours, even empty vessels; borrow not a few.

2 Kings 4:1-3

4. *Delays occur to test your faith.* The two blind men followed Jesus from the ruler's house to His own house before they had their miracle. They were shouting to Jesus to heal them but He ignored them. Finally, He turned round after they had followed Him on the long journey to His house. He asked them, "Do you believe?" Obviously, He could have healed them outside Jairus' house. He wanted to be sure that the two blind men believed in His healing power before He healed them.

And when Jesus departed thence, two blind men followed him, crying, and saying, Thou Son of David, have mercy on us. And when he was come into the house, the blind men came to him: and Jesus saith unto them, Believe ye that I am able to do this? They said unto him, Yea, Lord. Then touched he their eyes, saying, According to your faith be it unto you. And their eyes were opened; and Jesus straitly charged them, saying, See that no man know it.

Matthew 9:27-30

5. *Delays occur in order produce patience in you.* Every time your faith is tested, it produces patience because faith always works together with patience.

Knowing this, that the trying of your faith worketh patience.

James 1:3

6. Delays occur to test your ability to endure shame. The word, "importunity" used in the Scripture below is actually the word anaideia which means "shamelessness." Without the ability to disregard shame, you will not be able to get far with God. Delays often produce shameful circumstances which you

have to endure. Perhaps there is a delay in acquiring a car, a husband or a child. You may have to struggle without one and endure the attitudes and impressions of people around.

And he from within shall answer and say, Trouble me not: the door is now shut, and my children are with me in bed; I cannot rise and give thee. I say unto you, Though he will not rise and give him, because he is his friend, yet because of his importunity he will rise and give him as many as he needeth.

Luke 11:7-8

7. *Delays occur to test your persistence.* Persistence is an important quality that reveals the extent to which you believe in something. You may believe in something but having to persist in blind faith will test your beliefs.

And he from within shall answer and say, Trouble me not: the door is now shut, and my children are with me in bed; I cannot rise and give thee. I say unto you, Though he will not rise and give him, because he is his friend, yet because of his importunity he will rise and give him as many as he needeth.

Luke 11:7-8

8. *Delays occur to give you a chance to bear fruit.* In the story below, the owner of the vineyard decided to delay the cutting down of a tree by a year, in order to give it a chance to bear fruit. Sometimes, a delay in your life is God's window of opportunity for you to step into certain aspects of ministry.

He spake also this parable; A certain man had a fig tree planted in his vineyard; and he came and sought fruit thereon, and found none. Then said he unto the dresser of his vineyard, Behold, these three years I come seeking fruit on this fig tree, and find none: cut it down; why cumbereth it the ground? And he answering said unto him, Lord, let it alone this year also, till I shall dig about it, and dung it: And if it bear fruit, well: and if not, then after that thou shalt cut it down.

Luke 13:6-9

Chapter 57

What Ministry Is Like When God Does Not Help You

There was a great famine in Samaria; and behold, they besieged it, until a donkey's head was sold for eighty shekels of silver, and a fourth of a kab of dove's dung for five shekels of silver.

As the king of Israel was passing by on the wall a woman cried out to him, saying, "Help, my lord, O king!"

He said, "If the LORD does not help you, from where shall I help you? From the threshing floor, or from the wine press?"

2 Kings 6:25-27 (NASB)

The cry of the king was, "If the LORD does not help you, from where shall I help you?" This must be the cry of every pastor and shepherd. This must the heart belief of every pastor, that: If God does not help me no one can help me!

If this is what a pastor believes, it will show in many ways. If you believe that God can help you, you will find yourself praying a lot. You will find yourself studying the Word! You will find yourself waiting on God for long hours. This will be because you know that, "If God does not help you no one will help you."

You would have thought that someone in ministry would know that his help really comes from the Lord. But sometimes, it is pastors who rather have little time to wait on God. **The greatest secret of ministry is the secret of waiting on God.** From Him, all your help shall come! Try waiting on God for a day. Set aside a whole day and try praying for seven continuous hours. You will discover that the help of God is what makes the difference in ministry. Throughout your earthly life and ministry, waiting on God must be a priority that is never compromised.

Seven Descriptions of Life without God's Help

I want you to know what it will be like if God does not help you. I want you to have a picture of what ministry will be like if you do not wait on God. Hannah spoke of how people were destroyed when God did not help them. She knew from first-hand experience that without the help of God, she would not make it. She knew what it was like to be without the help of God. She knew what it was like when God was against you.

1. When God does not help, even mighty men are destroyed.

AND HANNAH PRAYED, AND SAID, My heart rejoiceth in the Lord, mine horn is exalted in the Lord: my mouth is enlarged over mine enemies; because I rejoice in thy salvation.

There is none holy as the Lord: for there is none beside thee: neither is there any rock like our God.

Talk no more so exceeding proudly; let not arrogancy come out of your mouth: for the Lord is a God of knowledge, and by him actions are weighed.

THE BOWS OF THE MIGHTY MEN ARE BROKEN, and they that stumbled are girded with strength.

1 Samuel 2:1-4

2. When God does not help you, people will not place much value on you or your ministry. You will not be rewarded with much more than bread for your services.

THEY THAT WERE FULL HAVE HIRED OUT THEMSELVES FOR BREAD; and they that were hungry ceased: so that the barren hath born seven; and she that hath many children is waxed feeble.

1 Samuel 2:5

3. If God does not help you, you will grow weaker instead of stronger.

They that were full have hired out themselves for bread; and they that were hungry ceased: so that

229

the barren hath born seven; and SHE THAT HATH MANY CHILDREN IS WAXED FEEBLE.

1 Samuel 2:5

4.   If God is against your ministry, you will die.

The LORD killeth, and maketh alive: he bringeth down to the grave, and bringeth up.

1 Samuel 2:6

5.   If God does not help you, you will be become poor.

The LORD MAKETH POOR, and maketh rich: he bringeth low, and lifteth up.

1 Samuel 2:7

6.   If God does not help you, you will be demoted.

The Lord maketh poor, and maketh rich: HE BRINGETH LOW, and lifteth up.

1 Samuel 2:7

7.   If God does not help you, the voice of your ministry will be silenced.

He will keep the feet of his saints, AND THE WICKED SHALL BE SILENT IN DARKNESS; for by strength shall no man prevail.

1 Samuel 2:9

Chapter 58

What It Is Like When
God Promotes You

God has promised to enlarge and to promote His servants. He will increase you and prosper you. Whatsoever you sow you shall reap. It was such a burden on the heart of the Lord for His sheep to be nurtured and cared for.

"Feed my sheep!" was the last passionate instruction from the Lord to His disciples. Surely, there must be a reward for obeying something so dear to the Lord's heart.

Faith is important in the ministry. A pastor must be a man of faith. You must have great expectations for church growth. You must believe that God will take care of you and increase the flock. You must look up and expect the Lord's blessings on the work of your hands. Without faith, it is impossible to please God! You are more pleasing to God when you believe that He will bless you and reward you.

God has promised to help and promote you. All through the Bible, God promises to help His servants in one way or another. Do not be afraid that your ministry will fail. God will lift you up and strengthen you so that you finish your calling. You may have many troubles, problems and issues but in the end, you will overcome them all.

I want to share with you several different promises from the Scriptures that you must hold on to. They are promises that speak of your future. These are predictions of the eventual outcome of your life and ministry.

Thirty-Eight Promises of Promotion

1. God has promised that you will break through.

   For THOU SHALT BREAK FORTH on the right hand and on the left; and thy seed shall inherit the Gentiles, and make the desolate cities to be inhabited.
   Isaiah 54:3

2. God has promised that you will not be ashamed and confounded. God has promised that you will not remember your season of widowhood (desolation) in ministry.

   Fear not; for THOU SHALT NOT BE ASHAMED: neither be thou confounded; for thou shalt not be put to shame: for thou shalt forget the shame of thy youth, and shalt not remember the reproach of thy widowhood any more.
   Isaiah 54:4

3. God has promised to gather you together with your flock.

   ...but with great mercies will I gather thee.
   Isaiah 54:7

4. God has promised that you will receive His mercy and His kindness.

   ...but with everlasting kindness will I have mercy on thee...
   Isaiah 54:8

5. God has promised that your children shall be taught of the Lord and shall have peace.

   And all thy children shall be taught of the LORD; and great shall be the peace of thy children.
   Isaiah 54:13

6. God has promised that you will be established in righteousness.

   In righteousness shalt thou be established...
   Isaiah 54:14

7. God has promised that you will not be oppressed.

    ...THOU SHALT BE FAR FROM OPPRESSION...

    Isaiah 54:14

8. God has promised that you will be removed from terror and fear.

    ...for THOU SHALT NOT FEAR: and from terror; for it shall not come near thee.

    Isaiah 54:14

9. God has promised that every weapon against your life shall fail.

    No weapon that is formed against thee shall prosper...

    Isaiah 54:17

10. God has promised that you will have superior power over accusers, liars, backbiters.

    ...and every tongue that shall rise against thee in judgment thou shalt condemn...

    Isaiah 54:17

11. God has promised to set you above all your colleagues.

    ...the LORD thy God will set thee on high above all nations of the earth:

    Deuteronomy 28:1

12. God has promised to bless you everywhere you go.

    Blessed shalt thou be in the city, and blessed shalt thou be in the field.

    Deuteronomy 28:3

13. God has promised to bless your children and livestock.

    Blessed shall be the fruit of thy body, and the fruit of thy ground, and the fruit of thy cattle, the increase of thy kine, and the flocks of thy sheep.

    Deuteronomy 28:4

14. God has promised to bless your possessions.

Blessed shall be thy basket and thy store.

Deuteronomy 28:5

15. God has promised you His blessings in your travels.

Blessed shalt thou be when thou comest in, and blessed shalt thou be when thou goest out.

Deuteronomy 28:6

16. God has promised to scatter your enemies.

The Lord shall cause thine enemies that rise up against thee to be smitten before thy face: they shall come out against thee one way, and flee before thee seven ways.

Deuteronomy 28:7

17. God has promised to bless the work of your hands.

The LORD shall command the blessing upon thee in thy storehouses, and in all that thou settest thine hand unto; and he shall bless thee in the land which the LORD thy God giveth thee.

Deuteronomy 28:8

18. God has promised that He will separate you unto Himself.

The LORD shall establish thee an holy people unto himself, as he hath sworn unto thee, if thou shalt keep the commandments of the LORD thy God, and walk in his ways.

Deutronomy 28:9

19. God has promised to make your blessings obvious to all.

And all people of the earth shall see that thou art called by the name of the LORD; and they shall be afraid of thee.

Deuteronomy 28:10

20. God has promised to make you fruitful.

And the LORD shall make thee plenteous in goods, in the fruit of thy body, and in the fruit of thy cattle, and in the fruit of thy ground, in the land which the LORD sware unto thy fathers to give thee.

Deuteronomy 28:11

21. God has promised to give you abundance so that you will lend to others.

The LORD shall open unto thee his good treasure, the heaven to give the rain unto thy land in his season, and to bless all the work of thine hand: and thou shalt lend unto many nations, and thou shalt not borrow.

Deuteronomy 28:12

22. God has promised that you will excel.

And the LORD shall make thee the head, and not the tail; and thou shalt be above only, and thou shalt not be beneath; if that thou hearken unto the commandments of the LORD thy God, which I command thee this day, to observe and to do them:

Deuteronomy 28:13

23. God has promised that your heart will rejoice in the Lord.

...My heart rejoiceth in the LORD...

1 Samuel 2:1

24. God has promised to make you a man of authority.

...mine horn is exalted in the LORD...

1 Samuel 2:1

25. God has promised that you will overcome and be able to speak boldly about past problems and enemies.

...my mouth is enlarged over mine enemies...

1 Samuel 2:1

26. God has promised that you will rejoice in the salvation of the Lord.

   ...because I rejoice in thy salvation.

   1 Samuel 2:1

27. God has promised that He will be your defence.

   ...neither is there any rock like our God.

   1 Samuel 2:2

28. God has promised that you will receive strength, even when you stumble.

   ...they that stumbled are girded with strength.

   1 Samuel 2:4

29. God has promised that you will not suffer from hunger anymore.

   ...and they that were hungry ceased...

   1 Samuel 2:5

30. God has promised that He will deliver you from barrenness and make you fruitful.

   ...so that the barren hath born seven...

   1 Samuel 2:5

31. God has promised that He will keep you alive.

   The LORD killeth and maketh alive...

   1 Samuel 2:6

32. God has promised that He will lift you up.

   ...he bringeth down to the grave and bringeth up...

   1 Samuel 2:6

33. God has promised that He will enrich you.

   The LORD maketh poor, and maketh rich...

   1 Samuel 2:7

34. God has promised that He will lift you higher.

   ...he bringeth low, and lifteth up.

1 Samuel 2:7

35. God has promised that He will raise you up from the dust.

   He raiseth up the poor out of the dust...

1 Samuel 2:8

36. God has promised that He will cause you to fellowship with princes.

   ...and lifteth up the beggar from the dunghill, to set them among princes, and to make them inherit the throne of glory...

1 Samuel 2:8

37. God has promised that He will direct your paths.

   He will keep the feet of his saints...

1 Samuel 2:9

38. God has promised that He will strengthen you.

   ...and he shall give strength unto his king, and exalt the horn of his anointed.

1 Samuel 2:10

Notes

1. W. Phillip Keller, *A Shepherd Looks at Psalm 23* (Grand Rapids, Michigan: Zondervan, 2007), 41-42.

2. Ibid., 58, 60, 66.

3. Ibid., 70-71, 73-74, 76-79.

4. Ibid., 84-85, 88.

5. Ibid., 61-62, 86-88.

6. Ibid., 98, 100, 103-105.

7. Ibid., 36-38.

8. Ibid., 113-115, 117.

9. Ibid., 120-121, 123-124.

10. Ibid., 129-131.

11. Ibid., 138-143.

12. Ibid., 150-152.

13. Ibid., 167-170.